Christian
Anthropology and Ethics

JAMES M. CHILDS, JR.

FORTRESS PRESS
PHILADELPHIA

Library of Congress Cataloging in Publication Data

Childs, James M   1939–
   Christian anthropology and ethics.

   Includes bibliographical references and index.
   1. Man (Christian theology) 2. Eschatology.
3. Christian ethics—Lutheran authors. I. Title.
BT701.2.C47   241   77–78626
ISBN 0–8006–1316–3

6440I77   Printed in the United States of America   1-1316

For Susan

Contents

Acknowledgments

This study grows out of eight years of personal research and teaching in the areas of contemporary theology and Christian ethics. Throughout this period of the book's germination and growth, I have been privileged to have had the feedback, encouragement, and above all, friendship of students and colleagues at a most remarkable institution, Concordia Senior College, Fort Wayne, Indiana. Concordia has for twenty years maintained a unique, upper-level pretheological liberal arts program. An educational enterprise of this sort places one at the intersection of theology and culture. This is particularly fertile ground for the study of theology and ethics in the service of the church's ministry in the world. I will be forever grateful to the Concordia community for some of the best and richest years of my life. I have experienced the eschatological values of which I speak in theological and ethical terms throughout this book as concrete realities among the people of this community. Unfortunately, as I write these words, Concordia Senior College is on the brink of its own eschaton as an institution, the victim of a tragic parochial controversy. Theological attitudes which grow out of some of the problems of the tradition dealt with in this work have played no small role in the college's undoing. I am glad, therefore, that I have come to the completion of this project at this particular point in history.

I am grateful to others as well. My friend and former teacher Carl Braaten of the Lutheran School of Theology at Chicago has been an invaluable source of help and encouragement. A special thanks is due my loving parents who have supported me personally and materially for many years right up to the present. My wife Susan to whom this book is dedicated has, together with my children, made inestimable contributions to my life and career. I have learned more about the "good" in being loved by them and in living with them than I have ever learned from any book I have read or could possibly write. A sincere expression of gratitude is also due the Aid Association for Lutherans whose several generous faculty fellowships have enabled me to pursue my researches and my work on this book.

Despite all this wonderful help and support, the book has its limitations. Some of these are due to space and selection; others are doubtless due to my personal finite capacities. In any case, I consider the work programmatic rather than final. I look forward to critical response and to the opportunity to pursue further many of its aspects in future endeavors.

Part One

The Heritage of
the Tradition

Chapter I

The Search for Man:
An Introduction

In its most general terms, this book is a study of the Christian doctrine of man* and Christian ethics in the context of eschatological theology. Recent developments in the rediscovery of biblical eschatology and apocalyptic have been finding systematic expression in the work of such men as Wolfhart Pannenberg, Jürgen Moltmann, and Carl Braaten. An impressive corpus of constructive theology has already emerged from the eschatological perspective, sometimes known as the "theology of hope" or the "theology of the future." What has not been so extensively dealt with are various facets of the Christian doctrine of man and corollary efforts in the field of Christian ethics.[1] What I am attempting to do here, then, is to plot some of the contributions that eschatological theology can make toward both the contemporary understanding of man and the explication of the Christian ethic. The choice of these two focal points is not arbitrary. Christian anthropology and ethics belong together. Although there are other avenues of approach to the theological foundation of the Christian ethic, a clearly articulated understanding of the "authentically human" and the "human good" is essential. Moreover, it seems doubly essential in view of the fact that in our modern world the manifold ideas about the nature of man represent a considerable shift from those of the past.

THE PROBLEM OF THE PAST

In recent Christian ethics it has become popular to speak of the thrust of the Christian ethic as "humanizing" the world. This idea,

---

*Throughout the book the term "man" is used as the equivalent of "human being." This is customary in theological and philosophical discussions.

while constituting a new rhetorical and apologetic locution, is, of course, not a new concept at all. It is clear that the Judeo-Christian tradition since its inception has thought of God's gracious activity and man's ethical response in terms of the redemption and fulfillment of mankind. In Jesus, the Christ, true God and true man, both his salvatory work and his ethical example of *agape*-love constitute the zenith of this long tradition. Consequently, one would think that Christian ethicists would have a clear idea of what the authentically "human" or the "human good" is that our ethic strives toward in humanizing the world. Presumably, they do, for the most part. However, when one looks at the history of Christian thought up to the present time, one is struck by the variety of outlooks regarding how the gospel brings about the fulfillment of the nature and destiny of man and how the church ought to function to that end.

As H. Richard Niebuhr's modern classic *Christ and Culture*[2] makes clear, the salvation and fulfillment of man are understood sometimes in terms of his other-worldly destiny and sometimes in terms of his this-worldly development. Although Niebuhr's purposes are broader than my immediate interest in the nature and destiny of man, the viewpoints he records on the church's relation to the world and its culture are indicative of a variety of outlooks on man. The "Christ against Culture" position surely illustrates the other-worldly bias in the extreme. From Tertullian's antipathy to philosophy down through the monastic movement to the left wing of the Reformation, this approach favors a radical separation between all that is Christian and all that is secular or historical. Our world is a fallen world, hopelessly stained with sin and something to be avoided as a clear and present danger to the integrity of the holy community, whose proper home is heaven. Since nothing can be expected by way of creative change or progress within the pale of history, the appropriate ethic is one of withdrawal and preparation for the world to come. The Christian ethic is the personal ethic of the redeemed in a church that earns its name by evidencing its holiness and wholly otherness. By contrast, the "Christ of Culture" position integrates Christianity's message with the noblest aspirations and profoundest insights of enlightened human culture. In our own century the optimistic, this-worldly view of man implicit in this outlook has issued in a vigorous commitment to social action and trans-

formation. This is amply illustrated by the accommodation of Christ
and culture that took shape in the social gospel and various forms
of Christian humanism in nineteenth century liberal theology and
in contemporary secular theologies.

Of course, neither of these extremes has dominated the mainstream
of Christian thinking through the ages. Most often, the church in its
mission and ministry has tried to strike a balance in its concern
for both the other-worldly and this-worldly dimensions of the human
good. This third approach falls under Niebuhr's general heading
of "Christ and Culture." There are several varieties identified here
but "Christ and Culture in Paradox" is perhaps the one that displays as well as any the delicate theological balance required. The
Lutheran tradition with its theology of the two kingdoms is the principal representative of this category. In brief, this well-known doctrine
teaches that, while God's governance extends over both the church
and the world, that governance differs in each case. There is a kingdom of the right and a kingdom of the left. In the kingdom of the
right to which the church belongs, God's lordship in the hearts of
his people is established directly through the gospel of his Son. In
the kingdom of the left he rules through the "orders" or the governing
authorities he has established in this world for its own preservation.
Christians live in both kingdoms at the same time but with no confusion of the two. In the kingdom of the left they pursue a vocation
of Christian concern for a high level of civil righteousness and justice
while yet obeying the authorities which God has established for the
human good. In the kingdom of the right, faith active in love shows
growth in personal virtue and love for neighbor. The secular authorities of the left should not attempt to intrude on the kingdom of the
right, and the church, likewise, should keep hands off the temporal
authority of the kingdom of the left.[3]

Properly understood, this scheme offers a genuine opportunity for
Christians to understand the mission and ministry of the church
and its individual members as one truly geared to the "whole man."
However, the history of its implementation indicates that the distinction between the two kingdoms has in fact often served as a
premise for noninvolvement in social action, abdication of responsibility for the structures of human history, and a restriction of the
relevance of the gospel to the eternal salvation of individual souls.

Consequently, concern for the human good in terms of man's historical existence is restricted to acts of mercy for the relief of suffering. The transformation of historical structures for the prevention of suffering and the increase of human well-being is not appropriate to the mission of the gospel in the world. In the minds of some, even acts of mercy are extraneous to the work of the church unless a conscious effort is made to combine them with a verbalization of the good news. Obviously, in this interpretation of two kingdoms thinking, the genuinely human and the human good ultimately reside above and beyond history, and priorities are set accordingly.

Regardless of whether or not one chooses to employ the concept of "humanizing the world," it is certain that the Christian ethic of love for neighbor in love for God will require a clear understanding of the human good or the true *humanum* as the goal of its striving. The heritage of the tradition in its attitudes toward the church's mission in the world and its relationship to the world gives evidence, both implicitly and explicitly, of a variety of outlooks on man. This further indicates that the search for man must go on. That is, each generation must discover anew and for its own time the nature and destiny of man as God has determined them from the beginning of creation.

THE PRESSURE OF THE PRESENT

In our own time the pressure for this search is enormous. The rapid developments in science and technology, medicine and psychology are challenging our basic understanding of the nature of man. The new alternatives to the traditional concepts of humanity are in some cases striking and frightening. B. F. Skinner's attack on the treasured notion that freedom and dignity are tangible and intrinsic characteristics of the human makeup is well known.[4] Obviously, were his views to gain ascendancy, a major overhaul in our concepts of ethics and the structures of life together would be indicated. Far less known but no less deleterious to our most cherished ideas about ourselves is the thesis proposed by scientist Dean E. Wooldridge in his book *Mechanical Man*. Wooldridge argues that all characteristics of human behavior and human nature are capable of explanation purely in terms of the normal operation of the laws of physics in inanimate chemical matter. As a consequence, our quaint Christian belief that personality, freedom of the will, moral sensibility, and religious inclination are somehow intrinsic endowments traceable to man's creation in the image of God is relegated to the category of myth. As one might expect, the corollary to this is that the ideas of divine activity in the world, a personal God, and an absolute right and wrong are also stripped of their validity and function.[5] Alternatives like those of Skinner and Wooldridge are surely extremes. Yet, it is equally sure, it seems to me, that their ideas represent a more general shift in man's perception of himself.

B. F. Skinner and Dean Wooldridge are but two isolated examples in the contemporary search for man. In the midst of competing claims on our self-understanding, Christian theologians today feel the same sort of urgency to frame an apologetic response as Reinhold Niebuhr felt when he wrote his great work, *The Nature and Destiny of Man,* earlier in our century. However, the task of doing this is not simply one of attempting to deal with views of man *per se.* The entire contemporary understanding of reality has to be taken into account. In the modern consciousness, one important characteristic is that men conceive of reality in terms of process and temporality. In marked contrast to the older interpretations of the cosmos as a statically ordered hierarchy of being, process and temporality are concepts that signal a vision of nature and history as open to development, to the emergence of novelty, and to the projection of purpose. In the nineteenth century flowering of these ideas, process was wedded to progress in the optimistic conviction that the future would ultimately bring the realization of the ideal. As we all know, the myth of progress was dissipated by the cruel events of the first half of our century. However, notwithstanding this corrective to the earlier lack of realism about human progress, the understanding of this world as one of process and temporality appears here to stay.

The difficulty that theologians find in correlating Christian anthropology with this sort of world view is easy to understand when we realize that traditional doctrines of man have been framed for the most part in terms of the static world views of the past. As we shall see in succeeding chapters, the history of Christian reflection on man has tended to see him in a dualistic fashion. In a variety of ways the *humanum* has been dichotomized in a manner that pits the ahistorical, supernatural aspect of his nature and destiny against the historical and natural, usually to the detriment of the latter. Thus, the problem of our theological past takes on another aspect under the pressure of present visions of reality. It is not only that the tradition has left us with a variety of outlooks on man, as I earlier indicated; it is also the case that most of these traditional formulations are tinged with a dualistic view of man that is ultimately ahistorical. Of course, one could simply rest content with what has been handed down and assert it polemically over against the developments of modern thought. However, beyond the sometimes spurious demand for relevancy in theology, there are solid reasons for responding in some positive way to the pressure of the present world view. The recent rediscovery of the truly historical character of biblical eschatology has called forth a rethinking of both ancient and modern concepts of eschatology. In contrast to traditional ideas of the eschatological kingdom as essentially beyond history and a return to lost origins, eschatological theology today sees the future kingdom as the fulfillment of history. It is the coming kingdom, revealed in Christ, exerting its power and influence in our history until the day of its ultimate coming. In contrast to the ahistorical, realized eschatology of some modern theologies, eschatological theology is genuinely historical and futuristic.

The concept which best describes this outlook is *prolepsis*. The term refers to an anticipation, a description of the future before it happens. I like to define it by saying that a prolepsis is the presence of the future in the present. In this view, eschatology is not simply realized or inaugurated or purely futuristic; it is proleptic. The expected, longed for, and promised eschatological future of God is revealed to our present in the resurrection victory of the Christ. He is the prolepsis of the coming kingdom of God. As the fulfillment of centuries of future hopes projected in the eschatological and apocalyptic traditions of Israel, the Christ is the zenith of God's self-revelation in history, the revelation of our absolute future. Indeed, it is only in the vision and promise of that which is coming that we have access to our fullest possible understanding of God and the nature and destiny of our becoming humanity. Thus, the orientation of eschatological theology is futuristic in terms of the dynamic of the proleptic. It does not see God as being the pinnacle of a static hierarchy of being. It does not see God as wholly other, eternal being over against historical reality. Eschatological theology sees God as the future of the world, proleptically revealed in the Christ as *true God*. Similarly, eschatological theology sees man's destiny neither as a return to lost origins nor as a salvation from history into eternity. Rather it sees that destiny in terms of a fulfillment of historical being in the arrival of the kingdom of God, a fulfillment of our humanity proleptically revealed in the Christ as *true man*.

These ideas await further elaboration and development as this work progresses. However, for introductory purposes it is sufficient for the present to identify these marks of eschatological theology as the basis for a lively correlation with the current vision of reality as processive and temporal. This apologetic enterprise has, of course, been under way for some time in the work of the so-called theologians of hope like Pannenberg and Moltmann. Their efforts are paralleled by those of men in philosophy and theology like Teilhard de Chardin, Alfred North Whitehead, Ernst Bloch, Martin Heidegger, and the process theologians. Each in his own way has worked deliberately with models of process and temporality together with an appreciation of the dominant importance of the future in current thinking on life and the universe.

However, the pressure of the present for a clearly articulated Christian anthropology is not restricted to competing ideas about man or the challenge of recasting traditional understandings in terms of current visions of reality. Developments in science and technology, medicine and psychology are also creating situations which make the need to be clear about our nature and destiny more urgent than ever before. Moreover, it is clear from several examples of these contemporary concerns that the way in which we understand the problems involved illustrates our peculiarly modern sense of inhabiting a world of temporal process that makes responsibility for the future incumbent upon us. That is, the problems of today have brought us to the unsettling awareness that we are, on the one hand, human beings with some sense of our humanity and, on the other hand, people still becoming in that humanity with an increased sense of our ability to shape that becoming. In the context of modern medicine and bioscience, James B. Nelson reflects this view in a concise fashion:

> Whether in the individual or in the race, our humanity is not a fixed static quality. As individuals it is perhaps more accurate to say that we are in the process of realizing our humanity. We are not finished products. So also as a race our human nature has a dynamic quality about it. New developments in the bio-medical fields pointedly raise the question as to what humankind is yet to become, and for the first time in history we do have the technological capacity to alter in significant ways the nature of human nature. In spite of this capacity for change and modification, however, there are certain qualities which we can claim as normatively human.[6]

Nelson therefore speaks of the necessity for defining what it is to be genuinely human. To understand what is truly human can guide us in determining what acts of medical manipulation do violence to the meaning and purpose of life and what acts of manipulation and avenues of research actually or potentially contribute to the preservation and fulfillment of genuine human life.[7]

Paul Ramsey makes the point in the Preface to *The Patient as Person* that the doctor attending a patient is attending a patient not merely as a *case* but as a person and, therefore, finds himself involved in his professional duties with a view of man and an understanding of the meaning of life.[8] Harmon Smith asserts throughout his book *Ethics and the New Medicine* that our decisions about the difficult problems raised by the rapid advance of medical science must be informed by a definition of human life that is more than simply biological.[9] Ian Barbour, in discussing the "wonders" projected for the future of mankind through genetic manipulation, has concluded that the criterion by which such efforts should be encouraged or proscribed is an understanding of man not only as a biochemical organism but also as a responsible self.[10]

From within the scientific community itself, Leon R. Kass has expressed the fear that an uncritical embrace of progress in medical science could well lead to voluntary self-degradation and dehumanization. As a curb against this possibility, he enters an impassioned plea that efforts in medical research and practice be tempered by an ongoing quest for the answers to the most difficult and fundamental questions of what is "the distinctively human" and what constitutes the "human good."[11] The late biophysicist, Leroy Augenstein, has made the point that we require a reassessment of the questions *What is man?* and *Why is he here?* ". . . for the biological scientists are giving us reason to ask, not only what man is, but the further question of what we would like him to be—and then are giving us the power to do something about it!"[12]

Even before developments in medicine and the biosciences began to evoke urgent questions about the nature and destiny of man, the march of modern technology was the source of many a troubled concern for the human condition. In the theological discussion concerning technology no less a luminary than Paul Tillich years ago joined with the protest of the existentialists in their critique of the depersonalizing force of a technological culture. Though rejecting the adequacy of the existentialists' solutions, Tillich appreciated their analysis of the technological threat. In the reality of such a thing as an "industrial society" we have our first clue to the essential problem. An industrial society is one almost totally characterized by the notion of man as *homo faber*. That man is *homo faber,* capable of manipulating the raw materials of his environment for practical purposes, is undeniable. Moreover, this capacity of man is a measure of the transcendence of his humanness over bondage to the natural order. Yet man is also moral man, man capable of I-Thou relationships, religious man, and so forth. It is when one of these various interdependent qualities in the structure of man's being becomes isolated and dominant that the whole structure of man's being is distorted. The human being is a centered whole to which all his functions are subjected. The imperialism of one special function leads to depersonalization, for the person is subjected to this function and, indeed, becomes this function. If the notion of *homo faber* is allowed to dominate the culture, then we have a world of means in which the individual himself becomes a means and the person is no longer the end of society.[13]

Christian ethicist Roger Shinn has made some related points in his analysis of the effects of technology on human self-realization. Shinn lists four basic obstacles to the realization of personal identity in a technological society. In the first instance, the organization of industrial society is described as a deliberate effort to make individuals expendable. Like the organization of the military, which assumes the expendability of individuals due to casualties, the coded job description and the assembly line are "designed to employ replaceable skills rather than irreplaceable persons." The second obstacle follows from the first. The increase of technological efficiency in the doing of work has eroded the meaning of work for countless people. When people are less useful and more troublesome than the machines that replace them, they can no longer understand themselves as producers and workers. The third obstacle to identity is the need for ever greater coordination and social controls in a huge and complex technological society. The result is that economically, politically, and culturally the individual is absorbed in a vast network of interdependencies that is too large for him to understand or identify with. Whereas once man could find his identity in the subculture, he is now being asked to find it in a global world of impersonal interrelationships created by mass technology. Finally, Shinn notes that in the industrial society a human being can easily be regarded as a thing. In economic and political life and even in the view of some of the behavioral sciences, people are increasingly regarded as objects of manipulation. When persons come to think of themselves as such, the likelihood of an identity crisis is very real.[14]

Analyses like those of Tillich and Shinn have become a commonplace response to the technological world view in recent decades. Others have sought to go beyond this sort of appraisal in offering a way for man to find a new understanding of his own humanity in the process of affirming and gaining control of his technology. Victor Ferkiss, in his book *Technological Man*, argues the thesis that a new "technological man" must be created if humankind is to be preserved. At the present time technological man does not exist. "Bourgeois man" is still at the helm of the vast proliferating technology of our time. His makeup is ill-suited for this and, as a result, he is destroying himself and the natural world he exploits. However, by contrast, "technological man will be man in control of his own development within the context of a meaningful philosophy of the role of technology in human evolution."[15] This new breed of humanity will be at home with science and technology; he will dominate them rather than be enthralled to them. The hope for this rests with the arrival of a new vision of the *humanum* which can be the source of ethical norms that will guide men in harnassing their own science and technology for the future good. Technological man will recognize himself as being a genuine part of the natural world. Therefore, he will also recognize his obligation to respect the fact that his superior complexity gives him a superior status in the natural world. Consequently, he will set himself apart from and above his machines and technologies which represent lower forms of reality. Thus technological man will understand his true place *vis-à-vis* the natural world and his true capability. He will exercise that capability to take control of his own evolution.[16] In essence, the ultimate task of technological man will be ". . . the task of finally finding himself, of fulfilling his role in the universe by becoming fully human."[17] Once more, the urgency of the search for man is underscored both by Ferkiss's assessment of the need to do so in the present situation and by the challenge to customary ideas about man which his projected vision of technological man presents.

What Ferkiss is saying here comes near to summarizing my whole point regarding the pressure of the present for a continued search for the *humanum*. Science and technology have created a situation which threatens the future of humanity. As with the startling developments in medicine and bioscience, this situation requires a renewed clarity concerning the nature of man that is responsive to the modern view of reality and productive of norms that can guide us in coping with the situation. For his own part, Ferkiss has suggested as a solution the creation of a new stage in the evolution of humanity called technological man. In so doing, he defines his understanding of humanity in terms that are typical of the present-day picture of man and his world as processive and holistic. This only serves to remind us of the problems encountered in attempting to apply the anthropologies of the past to the world of the present. First of all, the theologian-ethicist must sift and evaluate the variety of outlooks on human nature and destiny which the history of Christian thought presents. Beyond this he must cope with the tradition's strong tendency to define man dualistically and in terms of a static world view. The catholic substance of Christian anthropology in the past took form in the context of the world of the past. To preserve that substance, it must take a somewhat new form for the world of the present.

THE INSTRUCTION OF THE FUTURE

All that I have said thus far about the problem of the past and the pressure of the present as urging man's continued search has been to set the stage for what follows. What has been offered is a selected set of illustrations which seem to characterize the task of contemporary Christian anthropology and ethics. First of all, for Christian ethics to address the problems of today, it will have to rest on theological foundations that are responsive to the pressure of the present. Secondly, if Christian ethics and its foundations in theology are to remain true to "what has always and everywhere been believed," then it must operate in lively correlation with its own past. As I have already suggested, the approach that appears most promising in enabling the theologian-ethicist to satisfy both these demands is that provided by eschatological theology. From this perspective we are given, as it were, instruction from the future in our present task of the search for man.

I propose to conduct this search basically in terms of the doctrine of man as the image of God, the principal *theologoumenon* for Christian anthropology. The doctrine does not bulk large in Scripture or tradition. However, the paucity of references to it in the history of Christian thought should not cause us to underestimate the fruitfulness of this theological ground. In the Old Testament the term "image of God" is the designation which alerts us to the distinctive character of man's nature in the created order. In the New Testament, where we find that Christ is *the* image of God, we are alerted to the fact that, in Christ, this term refers to the distinctive character of man's destiny.

It may be argued that, since the *imago Dei* in itself appears to lack extensive content in its biblical development, its explication is most useful as merely a heuristic device that leads us into broader and more fundamental areas of theology which, in turn, supply needed flesh for an otherwise slender concept. However, even if it is fruitful in just that way, this in itself should be enough to justify pursuit of the notion. In any case, Emil Brunner was able to say concerning the biblical phrase "in his image and after his likeness" that "the whole Christian doctrine of man hangs upon the interpretation of this expression. . . . The history of this idea is the history of the Western understanding of man. . . ."[18]

Accordingly, the balance of Part One of this volume charts the heritage of the history of Christian anthropology under the notion of the image of God. The next chapter is my attempt to demonstrate what has already been suggested, that a major part of Christian tradition has construed the image doctrine in such a way that some form of dualism has resulted in its understanding of man. In one way or another the dualisms presented by various thinkers reflect a key problem of our past: the disparity between man's nature as historical being and man's nature in terms of his ultimate fulfillment. This discontinuity between historical reality and eschatological hope is more than the inevitable discontinuity between what man is and what he ought to be that is the product of our sinful nature. It is a discontinuity that verges on an ontological dualism in presenting an idea of human fulfillment that is ahistorical and radically other than the historical reality man experiences himself as being. The history of this duality in the Christian understanding of man is the history of "Dichotomized Man."

In sharp contrast to the second chapter, the succeeding one explores the principally modern phenomenon of "Secularized Man." The dualistic tension in so much of Christian thinking on the nature and destiny of man appears completely relieved in this outlook. Beginning with Schleiermacher, we have a perspective on Christian anthropology which is almost totally historical in character. Human nature and destiny *both* lie within the boundaries of history. Indeed, anthropology itself becomes the center of a theology that has largely been emptied of any transcendent other-worldly dimension. However, in terms of what Christians "have always and everywhere believed," this is too high a price to pay for mitigating the dualities of the tradition. Moreover, secularized man represents an attenuated doctrine of sin in combination with an unwarranted optimism concerning the human condition.

Chapter Four, "Theonomous Man," represents an understanding of man in the image of God which has its roots in Augustine and its modern explication in the work of Paul Tillich. Indeed, the chapter title consciously appropriates Tillich's concept of "theonomy." Man understood theonomously is man understood as created in a certain ontological communion with God. The image of God is the symbol which refers to this reality. Given this immediate and integral relationship between the being of God and the being of man, the God-man relationship cannot be thought of as a *heteronomy* in which the nature and destiny of man are determined and directed by the "wholly other" God as though he were an essentially strange and outside force. Such a tendency inheres to some extent in the dualistic versions of the image doctrine. At the same time, the idea of theonomous man also precludes the sort of *autonomous* view of humanity represented by the image of secularized man. As we shall see, the theonomous understanding of the image of God presents a view of man that mitigates in part but not entirely the dualities of the tradition.

Throughout Part One the suggestion is clear that we have a problem in understanding the nature and destiny of man that has not been fully solved in the history of Christian thought. However, it is certainly not my intention to suggest that the history of Christian thought is bankrupt or seriously deficient in its understanding of man in the image of God. To maintain such a position would tend to indicate a lack of trust in the faithfulness of God to lead his people into all truth throughout the ages. No theologian worthy of his calling would hold such a doubt as a working principle. Therefore, I have attempted to develop the best insights of the past in an appreciative fashion in order to demonstrate in my eventual reworking of the *imago* doctrine a healthy continuity with the theology of all ages.

Part Two sets down the biblical-theological considerations which point to an eschatological perspective on the Christian doctrine of man. The larger context within which this treatment finds its place is the recovery of biblical eschatology and the theological framework that results. This is dealt with in Chapter Five, "The Recovery of Eschatology." Here I have attempted to delineate briefly the basis and substance of the major themes which characterize eschatological theology or the so-called theology of hope. Against the backdrop of eschatological theology, the succeeding chapter, "The Image of God and Eschatology," details the biblical materials specifically related to the notion of man in the image of God. In this chapter I have sought to demonstrate that the biblical understanding of man is an eschatological understanding that correlates nicely with the larger eschatological perspective of the whole of Scripture. Chapter Seven, "Eschatological Man," then, gathers up the insights of the two preceding chapters in a restatement of the doctrine of man in the image of God.

In terms of the search for man, Part Two, as a whole, summarizes the "instruction of the future" which eschatological theology provides. I think it is evident, both implicitly and explicitly, that the thoroughly historical understanding of man, which this theology displays, is an insight that speaks directly to the questions raised by the traditional formulations of the Christian doctrine of man. It is my conviction that the peculiar insights of eschatological theology's understanding of the historicality of man and reality go a long way toward mitigating the dualities of past conceptions of the nature and destiny of man. In so doing, eschatological theology offers an opportunity to enter into correlation with the modern view of man in its stress on a holistic, processive, and temporal understanding of human existence. Consequently, we are given an alternative to the attempts of secularizing theologies to address the same problems, an alternative that is essentially faithful to the tradition in a way that secular theology fails to be. How all this can be so awaits detailed explication in the chapters themselves.

It remains, then, in Part Three to map out the implications of these efforts for the discipline of Christian ethics. Ethics is an ancillary discipline. It must be grounded in a theology. What I hope to achieve, then, is a close and consistent correlation between the theological foundations of the Christian ethic and its theoretical formulation. The edifice of normative ethical theory should rest squarely upon its theological foundations and rise naturally from them. All too often efforts in formulating normative theory for the Christian ethic neglect or even run counter to their theological antecedents. By the same token, many carefully laid theological foundations for the Christian ethic are never translated into the concrete components of a decision-making apparatus. If both pitfalls can be successfully avoided, a worthwhile contribution to the task of Christian ethics might possibly result.

Chapter II

Dichotomized Man

In the tradition of the church the treatment of the doctrine of man under the notion of the *imago Dei* is complex and inconsistent, constituting, potentially, a full-length study in itself. However, the decisive points in the development of this doctrine and the basic options that have emerged throughout the history of Christian thought are well known. Consequently, it will be possible, as a first step in this study, to give a decent account of the heritage of the tradition by discussing these major options as illustrated by their outstanding proponents. And among these, it can be readily argued that those represented in the present chapter have dominated Christian thinking about the doctrine of man in the image of God. The understanding of man they have left us could well be designated as *dichotomized man*.

In one way or another the thinkers I shall presently discuss have explicated the image doctrine in a form that supports a dualistic notion of the *humanum*. The dualities or dichotomies which have emerged here are really of two kinds. The first variety might be called *structural* dichotomies in which man's nature in the image of God is divided by definition into two parts: an abiding natural image (reason, freedom of the will, moral sensitivity, etc.), on the one hand, and a supernatural image that is lost in the fall, on the other hand. In tandem with this sort of dualism we also find the dichotomy in man's being that is created by an *ahistorical eschatology*. The stress on a primordial state of integrity to which we will be restored with the restoration of the image in Christ at the end of history has infused the history of Christian thought with a circular, ahistorical return-to-origins eschatology. None of these outlooks goes to the extremes of Origen's cyclical, Neoplatonic *Endzeit gleich Urzeit* correlation, but they all reflect this pattern of approach to history and eschatology.[1] The structural dichotomies belong to a category I shall designate as "Twofold Interpretations of the Image." In contrast to this are the attempts to overcome this duality in the definition of the image represented by those who fit the label "Theological Monism." As we shall see, thinkers in this category do not depart entirely from the structural dualism inherent in the twofold interpretations. Moreover, both categories operate with the sort of dichotomy that comes with an ahistorical eschatology of the kind just described. The important point in this analysis is that the two types of dichotomies, in effect, reinforce one another. The divided portrait of man which we receive ultimately influences our understanding of the human good toward which the Christian ethic strives in response to our Lord's *agape* imperative.

TWOFOLD INTERPRETATIONS
OF THE IMAGE

In discussing the doctrine of the image of God generally and this type of interpretation specifically, Irenaeus is of particular interest. In the first place, as Gustaf Wingren has pointed out, his central concern is the subject of man and becoming-man in Christ.[2] In the second place, since Irenaeus recorded his thoughts on the doctrine of the image at a time when this doctrine was not really a part of the growing corpus of Christian teaching, it might be said that he was the founder of the doctrine as a formal theological concept.

There is considerable agreement among scholars that Irenaeus taught a twofold interpretation of the image of God based upon the distinction between "image" and "likeness" as they appear in Gen. 1:26.[3] Of course, this exegesis has not stood the test of subsequent scrutiny but Irenaeus's theological conclusions have remained influential. The most straightforward statement of the way in which he understood image and likeness as separate concepts is perhaps in the following from *Against Heresies*:

> For by the hands of the Father, that is, by the Son and the Holy Spirit, man, and not "merely" a part of man, was made in the likeness of God. Now the soul and the spirit are certainly a *part* of the man, but certainly not *the* man; for the perfect man consists in the comingling and the union of the soul receiving the spirit of the Father ["likeness" or "similitude"], and the admixture of that fleshly nature which was molded after the image of God. . . . when the spirit here blended with the soul is united to God's handiwork, the

man is rendered spiritual and perfect because of the outpouring of the Spirit, and this is he who was made in the image and likeness of God. But if the Spirit be wanting to the soul, he who is such is indeed of an animal nature, and being left carnal, shall be an imperfect being, possessing indeed the image (of God) in his formation, but not receiving the similitude through the Spirit; and thus is this being imperfect.[4]

For Irenaeus, then, the union of the body and soul is understood as constituting man's natural makeup in the *image* of God. The *likeness* or *similitude,* which perfect man also possesses, is a product of the outpouring of the Spirit in man's spirit.

From other passages in Irenaeus's writings it is also clear that the concept of the image basically refers to man's peculiar natural endowments of freedom and reason. These are not lost in the fall into sin but remain as characteristic of the *humanum*.[5] In distinction from the image, man's being in the likeness of God must be considered in some sense a supernatural gift.[6] This is implicit in the previous quotation. It is also implicit that this likeness can be and indeed is lost to sin and can only be restored in Christ by grace. Therefore, Irenaeus says of Christ's work that ". . . he both showed forth the image truly, since he became himself what was his image; and he reestablished the similitude after a sure manner, by assimilating man to the invisible Father through the means of the visible Word."[7] In sum, Irenaeus's twofold expression of the image doctrine includes the *image,* which refers to man's body and soul and especially his reason and freedom, and the *likeness*, which is a supernatural gift of the indwelling of God's Spirit in man's spirit. The former abides despite sin; the latter is lost to sin but restored in Christ.

We have here the rudiments of a dualistic view of man which dichotomizes between nature and grace or between nature (image) and supernature (likeness). For Emil Brunner the latter corresponds to the original righteousness (*justitia originalis*), a supernatural gift of grace added to man's nature which grants supernatural communion with God. Thus, he sees in Irenaeus the source of the Scholastic Roman Catholic dichotomy between the remaining image in natural man, which leaves man's freedom of the will intact, and the image which was lost, the original gift of grace added to man's nature (*donum gratia superadditum*).[8] Here we have our first illustration of a *structural* dichotomy.

Beyond this, as indicated earlier, Irenaeus was centrally concerned with man and becoming-man in Christ. It is finally in connection with our destiny in Christ, with soteriology and eschatology, that Irenaeus develops his theology of man in the image and likeness of God. His special vehicle for discussing soteriology and eschatology is, of course, his well-known concept of *recapitulation*. Irenaeus employs this notion in connection with a number of theological concerns. However, of immediate interest to this discussion is his idea that recapitulation refers to a restoration of what was lost in Adam's sin. The following two quotations express the matter concisely:

> . . . when He became incarnate, and was made man, He commenced afresh [other versions have "recapitulated"] the long line of human beings, and furnished us, in a brief, comprehensive manner, with salvation; so that what we had lost in Adam—namely, to be according to the image and likeness of God—that we might recover in Christ Jesus.[9]

> Thus, then, was the Word of God made man . . . God recapitulated in Himself the ancient formation of man, that He might kill sin, deprive death of its power, and vivify man; . . .[10]

What we have in Irenaeus's soteriology would appear to be an eschatology of return to lost origins. We have hints of this circular pattern of restoration in certain of the Greek Fathers[11] and in Justin Martyr, whom Irenaeus credits with the idea.

Gustaf Wingren in his study of Irenaeus's theology, *Man and the Incarnation,* also acknowledges this restoration pattern but contends, at the same time, that Irenaeus represents another kind of eschatological thrust. In contrast to the cyclical pattern of return-to-origins, one can also demonstrate that Irenaeus held a futuristic eschatology in which the Christ event brings to *fulfillment* or *perfection* the creation which was imperfect or incomplete at its beginning. Wingren's evidence and argumentation are persuasive and will demand our further attention at a later point in this study. However, in terms of the subsequent history of Christian thought, it is fair to say that the church did not pick up this genuinely "historical" aspect of Irenaeus's eschatology. Rather, it is truer to say that the church embraced and developed the understanding of recapitulation after the pattern of loss and recovery and that this, in turn, fostered a dualistic tendency in Christian anthropology by identifying man's true humanity as something outside history—before history in its original state and after history in the eschaton of restoration—

which, then, stands over against human nature as it exists in historical experience. This "historical-eschatological duality" in man's nature and destiny works in tandem with the structural duality discussed earlier to produce a divided understanding of humanity: natural *vis-à-vis* supernatural and historical *vis-à-vis* suprahistorical.

Irenaeus's general scheme was echoed in the thought of Clement of Alexandria[12] but it found its most comprehensive systematic expression in the later theology of Thomas Aquinas.[13] Following the anthropology of Aristotle's metaphysics, Aquinas asserts that man is the image of God because he, of all the creatures, possesses intelligence and understanding. The endowment of reason, then, is the basic content of the *imago Dei*. It is the possession of all men, and it represents the capacity for the natural knowledge of God and for seeking the highest good.[14] This unique ontic power of the natural man remains always, although it is damaged by sin.

However, although the notion of rationality dominates Thomas's entire discussion of the image doctrine, if we press further into the *Summa* we find that the image is ultimately a three-stage structure:

> Thus God's image can be considered in man in three stages: the first stage is man's natural aptitude for understanding and loving God, an aptitude which consists in the very nature of the mind, which is common to all men. The next stage is where a man is actually or dispositively knowing and loving God, but still imperfectly; and here we have the image by conformity of grace. The third stage is where a man is actually knowing and loving God perfectly; and this is the image by likeness of glory. Thus on the text of the Psalm, *The light of thy countenance O Lord is sealed upon us*, the *Gloss* distinguishes a threefold image, namely, the image of *creation, of re-creation, and of likeness*. The first stage of the image then is found in all men, the second only in the just, and the third only in the blessed.[15]

Here, then we have the image in conformity with nature, grace, and glory.

It is in view of this three-stage formula that one begins to sense the duality of the Thomistic definition. On the one hand, we have the natural image and, on the other hand, we have the supernatural image, the image in conformity with grace and glory. Although the natural image endows man with the capacity for knowing and loving God, the supernatural image of meritorious love of God, which includes the virtue of obedience to him, is possible only through grace.[16] This grace, together with its capacity for the supernatural virtue of perfect love and obedience to God, was lost in the Fall. Consequently, while the natural image remains, the supernatural is forfeited. Since in Thomas's reasoning that which is natural to man's original creation cannot be destroyed by sin, it follows that the supernatural image is something added to man's original nature, a *donum gratia superadditum*.[17] This superadded gift of grace was needed in man's primitive state of pure nature in order that he might achieve the supernatural good. Thus, in the state of corrupt nature he needs to have this grace infused again that he might be healed and fulfilled as a human being.[18] The well-known Thomistic axiom that grace perfects nature applies here.

From this brief analysis it is possible to conclude that Aquinas's three-stage doctrine of the image displays what is essentially a two-story or twofold doctrine of man which divides his being according to nature and grace or nature and supernature. The one is a constant ontic reality, even though tainted by sin, while the other is ultimately only realized fully in beatitude. Aquinas accepts Aristotle's *animal rationale* account of man in the natural universe adding his own account of supernatural grace. Once more we have a sharply defined structural dichotomy with regard to the nature of the *humanum* that is, in this instance, in correlation with a comprehensive view of reality.

However, notwithstanding this duality in Aquinas's view of things, one should appreciate the fact that his system is bent on synthesis rather than dualism. Because the natural image is a basic component in all men, there is a common ontic structure in all humanity. As a result, both the dictates of conscience and the natural law, as objective components of the order of being, may be appealed to as self-evidently valid for all men, not only Christians, in areas as wide-ranging as personal, political, economic, and cultural ethics.[19] By nature man perceives and inclines toward the good in all these areas of concern, achieving it in some small measure proportionate to his damaged natural abilities. By grace, which perfects nature rather than destroying it, he ultimately realizes that good. Thus, in this system, man has the ability to understand his own existence and the reality in which he participates as ordered under God and finally fulfilled in the perfection of his relationship with God. In this fashion, Aquinas attempts a synthesis between nature and grace, natural image of God and supernatural image, natural existence and ultimate destiny. At the same time, nature and grace remain distinct and unconfused. The key is the axiom "Grace does not destroy nature, but perfects it."

However, notwithstanding the beauty of this synthesis, the Thomistic hierarchical view of reality undercuts it. Although all men, as rational men inclined to the good, are images of God and therefore subject to the claims of conscience and the natural law, men are also sinners who have lost the rectitude of the supernatural image and who, therefore, err in their conscience and cannot always perceive and accomplish the good of the natural law. Only with the addition of God's grace which restores the right reason of the original rectitude can good be achieved either penultimately or ultimately. The dispensary and repository of that grace is the church, and therefore it has authority to speak out definitively in all spheres of personal and public ethics. In response to this situation Helmut Thielicke has written:

> We need hardly point out what extraordinary vistas are hereby opened up for the Roman Catholic mode of world conquest, of cultural, political, economic and social action. We are certainly confronted by a clear and consistent chain of argument which leads from subtle distinctions between the original *imago* and *similitudo* to a conception of theological ethics and finally to the concrete programs and practices of Roman Catholicism in the sphere of public action. Neither the programmatic guidelines of the papal encyclicals nor the directions taken by certain Catholic political parties are conceivable without that original distinction.[20]

The synthesis achieved by the Thomistic hierarchical system thus turns out to be based, in Thielicke's view, upon the distinction between nature and grace that is implicit in the doctrine of the image of God. However, ironically, the authoritarian nature of the hierarchy exacerbates the duality of nature and grace even as it proposes to place them in synthetic relationship to one another. This becomes clear in Paul Tillich's critique of the Thomistic system in which he points out that by placing religion (the supernatural) and culture (the natural) on different "levels" in the hierarchy that is reality—religion, of course, being in the position of dominance—Thomas invites conflicts between the two levels instead of harmonious, theonomous interpenetration. The result is for religion to be tempted to exert heteronomous control and suppress the autonomous functions of culture.[21]

It is a corollary of this kind of authoritarian approach on the part of theology that those committed to it are led ineluctably into cultural conservatism. Paul Tillich recognized this fact early in his career when he fought for the cause of religious socialism in prewar Germany. According to Tillich, the Catholic system is a heteronomy based upon a central authority principle and, as such, could not help but resist the sweeping social changes represented by a movement such as socialism.[22] H. Richard Niebuhr has made a similar observation in his critique of the Thomistic system by explaining that the synthesist of Christ and culture finds himself in a position where he must defend not only the gospel but also the perpetuation of the culture with which he has effectively synthesized his theology. Thus, for Thomas and all who take his tack, the tendency toward cultural conservatism is endemic.[23]

Obviously, this conservatism has far-reaching effects upon the church's attitude toward social ethical concerns. However, I mention it here particularly because it is a concomitant to another source of the dualism that we are tracing in the Thomistic system. If man is divided according to nature and supernature, then this duality is reinforced by the eschatological orientation of Aquinas's theology. Because he accepts the idea of a primitive state of integrity in which man possessed the original justice which the superadded gift of grace conveys and because this perfect rectitude is not fully restored until the beatitude of eternal life, we have once more the restoration motif of return-to-origins. The dichotomy of supernature versus nature can now be understood also in terms of eternal glorious existence versus imperfect historical existence. When one couples this with the static vision of reality that the hierarchical Thomistic system portrays, one recognizes that the duality of history and eternity is intensified. Historical existence is discontinuous with suprahistorical existence. One's eschatological hope for fulfillment of the human good is finally the hope to be translated from the historical to the suprahistorical. Eschatology is therefore ahistorical.

The result of this orientation to historical reality will be a tendency toward cultural conservatism because the elevation of eternity over time tends to stifle hopes and efforts for progress within the structures of history. Such cultural conservatism correlates with the same tendency we have just observed as a consequence of the heteronomous synthesis of Christ and culture presented in the Thomistic system.

Thus, the full ramifications of the duality in the image doctrine, which divides man's being according to nature and grace, go beyond the narrow range of Christian anthropology to involve a comprehensive outlook on reality.

THEOLOGICAL MONISM

Theological monism is a position that really belongs exclusively to the theology of the Reformation. As the label I have given it suggests, it stands in contrast to the "twofold" doctrines of the image just reviewed. Representatives of this category seek to avoid dualistic interpretations of man by representing the image of God as a comprehensive, undivided concept referring to the whole man. *Imago Dei* in this outlook refers to a theologically defined relationship between God and man which is constitutive of man's being. It has its beginnings in Luther, whose insights are systematically articulated in the subsequent Lutheran tradition. John Calvin's doctrine is not unlike Luther's in this regard, and the same basic position is represented in modern times by Barth and Brunner, despite their differences from the Reformers and from one another. For the immediate purposes of this chapter it should be sufficient to look closely at Luther who pioneered this approach.

As we shall soon observe, Martin Luther developed his doctrine of man in the image of God under the influence of some of the leading concerns of reformation theology. However, the initial departure from the tradition which was to characterize Luther's position was the result of his exegetical insight. Luther rejected the twofold understanding of the image which, since Irenaeus, had been based on the notion that *imago* (*tselem*) and *similitudo* (*demut*) could be taken as two distinct concepts corresponding to these two different vocables in the Hebrew text of Gen. 1:26. For Luther, this text was a clear case of Hebrew parallelism wherein *tselem* (image) and *demut* (likeness) ought to be understood as complementary terms indicating a single idea.[24] As a consequence, Luther also rejected the medieval distinction between the natural and supernatural image which rested upon the bogus exegetical distinction between image and likeness.[25]

In its place Luther offers us a single concept as an explanation of the image of God which is purely theological in its expression. Although he makes the point that we cannot really know what the

image is in a firsthand sense due to its loss in the Fall, Luther is able
to describe it in the following manner:

> Therefore my understanding of the image of God is this: that Adam
> had it in his being and that he not only knew God and believed that
> he was good, but also lived a life that was wholly godly; that is, he
> was without fear of death or of any other danger, and was con-
> tent with God's favor.[26]

> Therefore that image of God was something most excellent, in
> which were included eternal life, everlasting freedom from fear, and
> everything that is good.[27]

For Luther, then, the image is not concerned principally with natural
ontic endowments like reason and freedom of the will nor is it concerned with an additional gift of grace which perfects this nature; it
is a thoroughly theological idea that refers to man's right relationship
to God. The image of God is man's *original righteousness*. This right
relation to God "is not something added to his human nature; it is
the core and ground of his *humanitas*. That was Luther's revolutionary discovery."[28] In further contrast to the Thomistic position, the
image of God as original righteousness means that "the nature of
man is again understood theologically and not philosophically, man
as man is once more a 'theological being'. . . ."[29]

As I indicated before, Luther's understanding of the image is
finally a result of theological concerns as well as of his exegetical
insight. In all his discussion of the image doctrine he seems obviously
concerned that the *imago Dei* not be construed in any way that will
allow sinful man some remaining ability to know and love God and,
therefore, to be able to contribute to his salvation. Aquinas's doctrine of the image left to man by nature the power of remembering,
understanding, and loving God. Indeed, he went as far as to say
that by nature men love God more than they love themselves. This
assessment of human capacities lies at the foundation of the syner-
gistic Scholastic theology against which Luther was contending. It
represents a posture that is antithetical to the central doctrine of
Luther's reformation: justification *sola gratia* and *sola fide*. Consequently, Luther's monistic understanding of the image as original
righteousness is accompanied by his conviction that this image is
necessarily lost in the Fall and man is left with no ability to contribute to his salvation:

> I am afraid that since the loss of this image through sin we cannot understand it to any extent. Memory, will and mind we have indeed; but they are most depraved and most seriously weakened, yes, to put it more clearly, they are utterly leprous and unclean. If these powers are the image of God, it will also follow that Satan was created according to the image of God, since he surely has these natural endowments, such as memory and a very superior intellect and a most determined will, to a far higher degree than we have them.[30]

However, notwithstanding Luther's monistic conception of the image, David Cairns has suggested that there may be two respects in which Luther slips into a duality in his definition after all. The first instance of this is in Luther's comments concerning a "public" and a "private" image. Here Luther is commenting on man's dominion over the earth. He indicates that Genesis is speaking of the "public" image when it speaks of man's creation for dominion. This image remains even in man's sinfulness. By contrast, the "private" image is that which Paul speaks of in 1 Cor. 15:49. The private image is identified with "goodness and justice" and has been lost in the fall into sin.[31] The second instance of apparent duality occurs in this same context. Cairns finds in some of Luther's remarks the suggestion that he believed a "relic" of the image remained after the Fall. After stating that Adams and Eve knew the Word of God and understood it prior to their fall, Luther goes on to say that, since their sin, "we have feeble and almost completely obliterated remnants . . ." of this knowledge. He says further that the image is "almost completely lost."[32] The point Luther makes in this context is that man is superior to the rest of the animals because of this remaining remnant of the image.

In fairness to Luther it should be pointed out that neither the duality of "public" and "private" images nor the duality implicit in the "relic" or "remnant" of the image as the distinguishing feature of *humanitas* receives any further development in his thought. His overwhelming emphasis is on the singular idea of the image as original righteousness, the right relationship to the Creator which was lost in the Fall. Nonetheless, these dualities do represent echoes of the sort of structural dichotomy in understanding the *humanum* that we have observed in Irenaeus and Aquinas. They represent the problem that constantly follows theological monism: If the image of original righteousness is totally lost in the Fall, then one is hard pressed to account for the distinctive characteristics of man's *humanitas* which are still evident and which appear to be a part of the image when the whole of the Old Testament witness is considered. The later Lutheran dogmaticians struggled with this problem and ended up with a duality of the image in the "proper sense" and the "wider sense" that is essentially like Luther's distinction between the public and the private image.[33] The Lutheran confessions make no such distinction nor do they speak of a "relic" of the image. However, the idea of some remainder of the image or something like a "public" image is implied by their doctrine of civil righteousness which accords to the natural man broad possibilities for knowing and willing the good.[34]

Thus, despite the fact that Luther and his followers successfully restated the image doctrine as a monistic, theological concept referring to man's relationship to God, an awkward structural dualism lurks in the background. This duality is further intensified when one considers the nature of man in the framework of Luther's eschatology. A study of Luther's theology by Kjell Ove Nilsson sheds some light on this. Nilsson points out that Luther's understanding of Adam in the paradise state suggests that Luther believed that the perfections of the original image of God were something that Adam possessed *in spe* (in hope). The image was therefore not fulfilled and could be described, even in the beginning, as an eschatological concept. Nonetheless, the image is still constitutive of the nature of man, without which man would not be man. Thus, there must have been in Luther's thought a sense in which Adam possessed the image both in *substance* and in *hope*. When we consider Luther's appraisal of fallen man, we find this paradox continues, though in a somewhat different fashion. The image of God is indeed something which belongs to man's nature, without which he would not be man, but, at the same time, something which concrete man is missing since the Fall. For fallen man the image is something he can therefore only hope to be through eschatological renewal in Christ.[35]

Nilsson suggests that the key to understanding this paradox is to see it in terms of a duality characteristic of Luther's doctrine of the image, a duality between the divine and the human. Man as image in accordance with his determination as to *essence* is man as "human," man on a plane with the animals. This "human" side of the image abides from the beginning as the *substance* of our humanity. The divine dimension refers to man as image in accordance with his relationship with God. This is undamaged before the Fall but also unfulfilled. After the Fall it is destroyed and is only completely fulfilled in Christ on the last day. Thus, the *imago* for both Adam and fallen man is something he has both in substance and in hope.[36] If Nilsson's understanding of Luther is correct, it would seem that the basic difference between Adam before and after the Fall is not that the pre-Fall Adam possessed the image fully in terms of the perfections of original righteousness, but that he held it undamaged in hope and his "loss" of the image in sin was therefore a loss of the right relationship to God necessary to his ultimate fulfillment as man —a loss that would mean the end of his being were it not for the renewal of that eschatological hope and possibility in Christ.

When Luther's teaching is viewed in this way, it is tempting to see in Luther a thoroughly eschatological doctrine of the image. That is, our hope for being perfected by grace through Christ is not a hope for the restoration of lost origins but rather a hope and promise that, because of Christ, God will *finish* what he *began* in creation by fulfilling the image in the eschaton, despite the intervention of sin as man's rebellion against God's purpose for him. We may once more hope as Adam could before the Fall. Such an interpretation would seem to accord with the following comments Luther makes on Gen. 1:26, comments which indeed play a large role in Nilsson's thesis:

> Moses, therefore, indicates to those who are spiritually minded that we were created for a better life in the future than this physical life would have been, even if our nature had remained unimpaired. Therefore the scholars put it well: "Even if Adam had not fallen through his sin, still, after the appointed number of saints had been attained, God would have translated them from this animal life to the spiritual life." Adam was not to live without food, drink and procreation. . . . His physical or animal life was, indeed, to be similar to that of the beasts. Just as the beasts have need for food, drink and rest to refresh their bodies, so Adam, even in his innocence, would make use of them. But what is added—that man was created for his physical life in such a way that he was nevertheless made according to the image and likeness of God—this is an indication of another and better life than the physical. Thus Adam had a twofold life: A physical one and an immortal one, though this was not yet clearly revealed, but only in hope.[37]

It would appear from this, then, that Luther's concept of the image

was an eschatological rather than a protological concept. Notwithstanding the hints of dualism in Luther's talk of man's physical life
versus his spiritual destiny, his remarks on Genesis allow us to conclude that, for him, eschatological existence in the image is not
opposed to or different from historical existence nor does it render
historical existence meaningless by postulating that the end of man's
destiny is a return to his beginning. Rather, eschatology is the fulfillment of protology. Given this insight, it might also be possible to
suggest that the dualisms of history and eternity and history and
suprahistory that typify restoration eschatology are mitigated in
Luther's eschatology.

In the final analysis, however, these insights concerning Luther's
eschatology strike a fairly minor chord in his thought. His overwhelming emphasis on a loss of the image together with his vivid
portrait of the perfections of the original paradise condition leads
him ineluctably into a restoration-type eschatology even as it led
him into the dichotomies of image and relic, public and private
image, and physical determination and spiritual determination. When
history is essentially fallen history and eschatology is a restoration of
that which obtained before fallen history, then there will be a fundamental opposition between man's historical being and his eschatological being; his destiny is discontinuous with his nature.

This dichotomy and discontinuity are reflected in Luther's two kingdoms theology, which I briefly described in the previous chapter. In
two realms thinking there is a dualistic tendency to concentrate the
ministry of the church on the inner man and to depreciate the value
of historical existence, for if historical existence is replaced by rather
than fulfilled by the eschatological kingdom, then little in the way
of meaningful change can be anticipated in history.[38] Paul Tillich's
critique of the two kingdoms tradition is telling in this regard.
Tillich labels it as a "transcendental" interpretation of the meaning
of history which is inadequate because it excludes both culture and
nature from the saving processes of history. This fundamental inade-
quacy is evident in that it contrasts the salvation of the individual
with the transformation of corporate historical structures; it contrasts
the realm of salvation with the realm of creation; and it interprets
the kingdom of God as a static supranatural order which individuals
enter after their death rather than a dynamic power in the process
of coming.[39] These inadequacies or contrasts which Tillich cites are,

of course, dichotomies which have their counterpart in the fundamental dichotomy between man's historical nature and his eschatological nature. Once more, we have an illustration of how Christian anthropology affects the Christian ethic and the church's outlook on its role in the world and in history.

In the final analysis, Luther's theological insights on both the image of God and the doctrine of the two kingdoms are sound, despite the presence of a certain dualism. There is a fundamental dualism we encounter in understanding the nature of man and the kingdom of God in relation to history. This is simply the dualism that exists between what man is in his sinfulness and what he ought to be in virtue of God's created purpose, as well as what he can be in God's creative grace. For this reason one cannot equate the kingdom of God and history any more than one can say that there is any sense in which natural, historical man is man as he ought to be. It is this profound truth, which the law of God convinces us of and which leads us to see our absolute dependence on grace, that Luther preserves for us. In his formulation of the *imago* doctrine and in his teaching on the two kingdoms Luther maintains this necessary and valid sort of dualism by dealing with the essence of man in terms of his relationship to God and by effectively contrasting the kingdom of God with the orders of history.

However, the dichotomies in the nature and destiny of man that are evident in Irenaeus, Aquinas, and Luther go beyond what is necessary to preserve the valid theological dualism just discussed. These fundamental dichotomies endemic to the outlook on reality shared, in some measure, by all three thinkers are those of nature and spirit, history and eternity. The question therefore remains as to whether or not the biblical materials which lie behind all their formulations really entail the maintenance of the dualities peculiar to their world view. Surely it is a world view very different from our own and one that produces a vision of the nature and destiny of man that is difficult to fit into man's current experience of himself. Is it possible to restate Christian anhropology in forms more appropriate to our present thought world? Is it possible to do so in a way that preserves the best insights of these great theologians and in a way that is faithful to the Bible? I believe the answer to both questions is yes. However, before an attempt can be made to demonstrate this, other options in the history of Christian thought must yet be considered.

Chapter III

Secularized Man

The dualities in understanding the nature of man which we have just observed display the tension between man's historical nature and destiny and his suprahistorical nature and destiny. When such a duality and tension exist, it is almost always to the disparagement and devaluation of the historical. In contrast to this mode of thought, the outlook I shall call "Secularized Man" elevates the historical over the suprahistorical to the virtual elimination of the latter. In this approach history becomes the proper locus for human hope and fulfillment.

Roger Shinn's characterization of the secular perspective captures this contrast nicely. He makes the point that an appreciation of the secular is an aspect of the new humanism of our time. It is ". . . an appreciation for the history in which we live as a realm of real possibilities and opportunities, not simply as a meaningless process or a preparation for a life to come. The ethos is that of a rejoicing in the world rather than a resigned endurance."[1] Behind the emergence of this secular spirit lies "a long history of the emancipation of man from the domination of heteronomous authority. . . ."[2] The secular outlook ". . . exults in human nature and in potentialities released from traditional inhibitions."[3]

The secularizing trend in Christian theology is normally identified with the recent appearance of books such as *The Secular City* by Harvey Cox and *The Secular Meaning of the Gospel* by Paul M. van Buren. However, as Shinn's remarks suggest, the appreciation for the secular so characteristic of our present mood has a long history behind it. Consequently, it seems appropriate, first of all, to delve a little into at least the more recent historical antecedents of twentieth century secularized man.

MAN IN THE CENTER

As a part of the tradition of Christian humanism, secularizing theology places man at the center of the theological task. Man's experience, his history, his institutions, and his culture are the touchstone and central focus of theological reflection. Therefore, any discussion of the immediate forerunners of contemporary secularity in theology should certainly include Friedrich Schleiermacher. Schleiermacher is well known for taking human experience as his point of departure for doing theology, and his discussion of the human makeup in this connection affords a ready contrast to the understandings of man as the image of God which we traced in the last chapter.

Although Schleiermacher refers to the *imago Dei* only briefly and in passing, it appears clear from his development of a Christian doctrine of man in the context of his understanding of religion that the "God-consciousness" or feeling of absolute dependence that is characteristic of man's religious makeup is his way of discussing many of the elements associated with the image doctrine in Protestant orthodoxy.[4] He rejects the notions of an original perfection of the world and an original perfection of man (original righteousness) which included immortality, as those ideas were traditionally understood. In general, he has difficulty accepting such notions because of the lack of an analogy by which we might conceive of an absolute-state-of-perfection-in-the-beginning. The terms perfection, righteousness, etc. are only understandable from the standpoint of relative history. So, for example, the very command to have dominion over the earth, which is associated in the tradition with the content of the image of God in its perfection, is in contradiction to the idea of a perfect primordial state. Dominion can only be understood as something resulting from a development of man's powers for the constitution of the world in the course of history.[5]

The case is similar when we try to conceive of a primitive man at all:

> . . . the first condition of man cannot be conceived as different from the later conditions which are determined by previous conditions; that is to say, an absolutely first condition cannot be conceived at all. Also, if we are unwilling to fall back on instinct, it is unthinkable that there should be consciousness of those created capacities before they are applied, and again it is inconceivable that, in a genuinely

human situation, there should be an impulse which would set them in motion without consciousness of them.[6]

In light of this, it is equally impossible to adopt the tradition's understanding of the image of God as the original perfection or righteousness of an actual first man.[7]

Rather, man's original perfection can be reconceived in terms of the God-consciousness:

> . . . so we account it part of the original perfection of man that in our clear and waking life a continuous God-consciousness as such is possible; and on the contrary, we should have to regard it as essential imperfection if the emergence of the feeling of absolute dependence, though not abrogating any feeling of partial dependence of freedom, were confined as such to separate and scattered moments.[8]

This God-consciousness of the original perfection does not, of course, refer to the peculiar quality of one primordial man who lost it in the Fall. It is both continuous and universal.[9]

If it is impossible for us to conceive of an absolute state of perfection in the beginning, it is equally impossible to conceive of an absolute first sin constituting the Fall and from thence imputed to all mankind. As all men share in the original perfection of the God-consciousness, so all responsibly share in the incapacity for the good which is original sin. At the same time, however, this congenital sinfulness should not be overestimated so as to deny man the capacity to appropriate the grace of redemption. The formulation which succinctly expresses Schleiermacher's understanding of these matters is that orginial sinfulness along with original perfection (God-consciousness) are timeless universal elements coexisting in the being of man. However, the dialectic of the two within the structure of man's being is not such that it is possible for any real active righteousness to emerge. There can only be ". . . a vacillation between vitiated spiritual efforts and increasing and fully matured sin."[10] Man is thoroughly in need of the grace of redemption.

Adam for Schleiermacher is a cipher for all men. If there is an ideal for humanity, it is not to be found in the image of God which Adam once possessed but lost. The ideal for human nature is rather to be found in Jesus of Nazareth who is the last Adam. Jesus Christ is the *Urbild*, and the *Vorbild*, the prototype and exemplar of ideal humanity in that in him the God-consciousness is regnant. Through the power of redemption which he communicates, men are formed as persons: ". . . he brings into focus in other selves the feeling of absolute dependence, the consciousness of sin and of the overcoming power of God, and the consciousness of the good-pleasure of God."[11]

In sum, we may deduce that, for Schleiermacher, the God-consciousness is that capacity of man which is inherent in the structure of his humanity and which replaces as a concept ideas about the original nature of man often identified in the tradition with the image of God. This deduction is buttressed by the observation that Christ, whom the New Testament, as we shall see later, sees as *the* image of God, is, for Schleiermacher as well, the *Urbild* and *Vorbild* of humanity, largely in virtue of his regnant God-consciousness. Schleiermacher's conception represents an understanding of the *imago Dei* as a capacity of man which is the measure of his humanity. The God-consciousness is a unique and autonomous aspect of the universal essence of mankind.[12] There is a God-ward thrust to this human quality but the stress is on certain capacities or endowments which are the peculiar possession of the human nature rather than on the relationship with God which they make possible. Indeed, H. Richard Niebuhr has pointed out that Schleiermacher fell victim to a temptation that has always plagued Protestantism with its strong emphasis on personal faith. He made the God-consciousness or feeling of absolute dependence his object of concern rather than the relationship with God to which it points. In this fashion he directed the attention of faith toward itself and in this sense we can speak of Schleiermacher's theology as one that places man in the center of its concern.[13]

Schleiermacher's thoughts on man as the image of God clearly do not lead him into a dualism in his understanding of the *humanum*. Since for Schleiermacher there is no such thing as a primordial state of perfection to which man hopes by grace to return, there is no danger of pitting man's nature suprahistorically understood against man's nature historically understood. Moreover, since there is no real notion of the loss of original perfection, there is, consequently, no problem of understanding how the abiding, universal image of God in man might be effected by what was lost in the Fall. As long as one holds that (1) the image refers to man's perfect original nature lost in the Fall and (2) that the image is also a reference to *humanitas* (the distinguishing characteristics of human nature that remain in all men), one is forced to the position that man must be understood on two levels: in terms of what he has lost to sin and in terms of what he still is in his nature as image of God. This is in part how the structural dichotomies previously observed come into being. A variation on this theme would be the idea of a partially damaged image which leaves man capable of the good in some regards but not in others. This too sets up a structural dichotomy in the human makeup.

Schleiermacher's position avoids both these pitfalls by simply asserting that the God-consciousness, his substitute concept for the image of God, is the single, key universal element in the human makeup. Man's nature and destiny from this perspective are to be understood not in terms of what once was and again may be by grace—we have seen that this scheme of restoration of lost origins is rejected by Schleiermacher—but rather in terms of what we may confidently expect it will be at the end of a universal, evolutionary spiritual process by which the God-consciousness becomes ever more regnant and pervasive through Jesus Christ.[14] In this process we come to see that the world is the scene of redemption and divine revelation. This conclusion, in turn, impels the church to see its mission largely in terms of the Christian ethic as a world-transforming force. Thus, toward the end of *The Christian Faith*, Schleiermacher is able to say:

> The divine wisdom, as the unfolding of the divine love, conducts us here to the realm of Christian Ethics; for we are now confronted with the task of more and more securing recognition for the world as a good world, as also forming all things into an organ of the divine Spirit in harmony with the divine idea originally underlying the world-order, thus bringing all into unity with the system of redemption. The purpose of this is that in both respects we may attain to perfect living fellowship with Christ, both in so far as the Father has given Him power over all things and in so far as He ever shows Him greater works than those He already knows. Hence the world can be viewed as a perfect revelation of divine wisdom only in proportion as the Holy Spirit makes itself felt through the Christian Church as the ultimate world-shaping power.[15]

In this way, Schleiermacher's anthropocentric theology is "history-centered" theology as well. That is, man's being is understood and appreciated completely in terms of the way man experiences himself in history and the fulfillment of man's being is understood in terms of the future development of history. There is no reflection on primordial past or suprahistorical future. There is, consequently, no division of the Christian ethic into two realms. Indeed, the Christian ethic, as active concern for the world as the arena of man's fulfillment, moves from the secondary position it held in the bulk of prior tradition to a primary position by its virtual identification with the process of redemption.

This same man-centered, history-centered approach to theology was developed and expanded by one of Schleiermacher's most prominent liberal successors, Albrecht Ritschl, who worked principally with the idea of the kingdom of God. In Ritschl's thought the effect of such a theological posture upon the role of ethics in the Christian life and mission is even more pronounced. For Ritschl the kingdom of God is a goal of history which is understood as the fulfillment of humanity in the attainment of a perfect society of persons. Thus, Ritschl writes:

> The Christian idea of the Kingdom of God denotes the association of mankind—an association both extensively and intensively the most comprehensive possible—through the reciprocal moral action of its members, action which transcends all merely natural and particular considerations.[16]

This vision is not unlike Kant's idea of a kingdom of ends and, like Kant, the key is man's ethical striving. As H. Richard Niebuhr has observed, Jesus' hope for the future breaking in of God's eschatological kingdom and his noneschatological faith in a transcendent God who rules heaven and earth in the present are both absent from Ritschl's conception of the kingdom of God. "All the references are to man and to man's work; the word 'God' seems to be an intrusion, as perhaps those later Ritschlians recognized who substituted the phrase 'brotherhood of man' for 'kingdom of God.' "[17]

Nonetheless, the idea of the kingdom of God is an eschatological idea, and Ritschl's merger of eschatology and ethics represents a major departure from the tradition. Norman Metzler has made this clear in a dissertation entitled "The Ethics of the Kingdom." Metzler observes that Ritschl saw the kingdom as both a divine gift and an ethical task; it was the religious and ethical highest good to be realized gradually in the course of history by the self-realizing ethical activity of man.[18] The problem with this formulation is that it is not self-evident from traditional theology that ethics and eschatology should be so closely related. Indeed, traditional dogmatics affirms the heterogeneity of eschatology and ethics. Eschatology is viewed as purely religious and other-worldly, referring to the kingdom to be realized by God alone at the end of time. Ethics is seen primarily as a worldly human enterprise. Ritschl veered to the worldly side stressing the priority of ethical striving, notwithstanding the fact that, paradoxically, he also held to a transcendent eschatological consummation as well.[19]

Ritschl's ethical-developmental scheme of the gradual realization of the kingdom of God in history came under attack by the exegesis of one of his students, Johannes Weiss. Weiss, along with Albert Schweitzer, discerned that the real context of Jesus' proclamation was the eschatological ideas of late Jewish apocalyptic. Weiss believed that Jesus' ethic was therefore eschatologcal in its rejection of all worldly goods and standards.[20] This viewpoint placed Weiss in the strongest possible contrast to Ritschl's primary ideas about the kingdom of God. Other students and followers of Ritschl, namely, Hermann, Harnack, Troeltsch, and Rauschenbusch, were aware of Weiss's critique and to some extent appreciative of his insights. However, none was able to work into his own theology any positive application of this eschatological critique to a modification or revision of Ritschl's ethical-developmental concept of the kingdom of God.[21]

The question remains as to whether the historical understanding of the kingdom of God so strong in Ritschl can be wedded to the eschatological understanding, which Weiss held Jesus taught, in such a way that the close relationship of eschatology to ethics can be maintained. To do so means an "historicizing" of traditional eschatology and an "eschatologizing" of history. Another way to put this would be to say that we need to eradicate the dualities in our understanding of man that set his suprahistorical nature and destiny over against his historical nature and destiny. Schleiermacher, Ritschl, and their nineteenth century followers resolved this duality by suppressing the suprahistorical and transcendent. They present us with a man-centered, history-centered theology that dissolves the Christian religion almost totally into an ethic of world transformation. In large measure, this posture appears helpful to the twentieth century search for man that I spoke of in the first chapter. It has the virtue of a this-worldly, historical orientation appropriate to the contemporary mind-set, and it virtually eliminates the dualism in traditional conceptions of man, which I indicated is so problematic for current apologetics. However, this liberal scheme embodies two theological problems which render it an unacceptable solution for responsible theology in any era. First of all, the suppression of transcendent, eschatological dimension in our understanding of man and history is too radical a departure from both the Bible and the tradition. The dualities of the tradition may be problematic in certain respects but in other more profound respects they faithfully mirror the proclamation of Jesus of Nazareth, the Christ. They express centuries of Christian hope in a transcendent God who in grace and power will bring his kingdom to pass. The critique of Weiss and Schweitzer and the subsequent reaction of neo-orthodoxy against the theology of nineteenth century liberalism were to be expected. Secondly, the ethical-developmental schemes of human self-realization to be found in both Schleiermacher and Ritschl reflect the optimism of their century's progressivist mentality. They fail to be cognizant of the one dualism I have already indicated as ineradicable: the contrast between what man was created to be and what he has made of himself in sin. Eschatology when understood as the divinely wrought fulfillment of man and creation stands in judgment against the pretenses of man's feeble efforts to attain the good in history. It need not devalue the historical *per se* but it cannot ascribe to fallen history the power for its own salvation.

THE SECULAR OUTLOOK

The centrality of man and history and the resultant emphasis on ethics, which we have just observed in the nineteenth century, continue to characterize the contemporary secular outlook. Naturally, a great deal of theological development has occurred, and significant differences between the theologians of secularity in the present and the liberals of the past are easy to record. However, my purpose here as elsewhere in this study is not to engage in comparative analysis of theological systems but to describe a variety of general outlooks on man. Therefore, while some distinctions must certainly be drawn between our various representatives, the primary interest lies with the common bonds they exhibit in viewing the nature and destiny of man.

E. L. Mascall in his book *The Secularization of Christianity* has suggested that there are three chief reasons for the secularization of

Christianity in our century. The first of these is the influence of positivism, especially as it has taken shape in the criticism of theological language by the linguistic analysts. The second reason, which Mascall believes is more pervasive, is the conscious and subconscious conviction that the supernaturalist outlook of traditional Christianity is incompatible with the modern scientific world view. The third reason is that the recent course of biblical scholarship, culminating with Bultmann, has consigned the supernatural to a mythopoeic vision of reality held by the early church.[22] Mascall's analysis offers us a convenient scheme for selecting representatives of the secular outlook. Paul van Buren illustrates the results of the first influence, Harvey Cox appears to reflect the second and, of course, Rudolf Bultmann is the consummation of the third. I think, however, that it is fair to say, before going on with this scheme, that to some extent all three influences have been operative in all three cases.

Paul van Buren's work has been analyzed and criticized exhaustively in recent years. This is of course true of Bultmann and Cox as well. Therefore, it should be sufficient in each case simply to capture some of the key thoughts which demonstrate their relevance to present purposes. Van Buren's basic interest in *The Secular Meaning of the Gospel* is ostensibly Christology. However, the manner in which he develops this interest makes it clear that he belongs in our discussion of secular man. The question van Buren raises for the book is, quite simply, "How may a Christian who is himself a secular man understand the gospel in a secular way?"[23] The "secular" outlook of secular man finds definition, we are told, only in the process of answering this question by determining the secular meaning of the gospel. The secular outlook represents a faith outlook.[24] However, it is clear that it is an empiricist and an atheistic outlook.

Such a determination can be made from the inherent presuppositions of van Buren's methodological commitments. He charts the course to the secular meaning of the gospel by way of linguistic analysis. Although he settles on an amalgam of approaches to the analysis of religious discourse that go beyond the radical attacks of early logical positivism, his reasoning belongs among its fruits. He rejects a cognitive approach to religious language, which would keep him within the theistic camp, in favor of a noncognitive "blik" (Hare) conception of religious statements as expressing commitments to a way of life.[25] This would appear to be a consequence of the fact that van Buren considers it necessary to the quest for the secular meaning of the gospel that the method of linguistic analysis used must adhere to the verification principle of logical positivism.[26] That principle, simply stated, requires that meaningful language must be capable of verification or falsification on empirical grounds. As is well known, in the early stages of linguistic philosophy analysts like A. J. Ayer were led by this criterion to the conclusion that theological statements were literally "non-sense." God-talk was relegated to the scrapheap of useless verbiage along with its closely associated moral utterance.

Obviously, van Buren does not want to say that theological language is without meaning. However, in his embrace of the verification principle and its concomitant notion of a noncognitive approach to the meaning of language, he makes statements that are surely echoes of the logical positivists: ". . . 'simple literal theism' is wrong and 'qualified literal theism' is meaningless."[27] And, "Today, we cannot even understand the Nietzschean cry that 'God is dead!' for if it were so, how could we know? No, the problem is that the *word* 'God' is dead."[28] Consequently, when one applies the razor of the verification principle to the language of the Christian faith, one cuts out the notion that "facts" are an integral dimension of this discourse. "Facts" are logically confusing to a language game that is primarily one of discernment and commitment.[29] "God-statements" need to be regarded as essentially "man-statements" or "statements about human existence."[30] Thus, van Buren's empiricist secularity results in the removal of the divine, the suprahistorical, the supernatural, the transcendent. Its concentration is on man and the peculiar commitment to a way of life that is the christological message of the gospel. Its understanding of man is one that is totally contained within the boundaries of finite nature and history. In short, we have a radicalized version of the tendencies to anthropocentricity and this-worldliness evidenced in the foregoing discussion of the nineteenth century liberals.

These features of van Buren's program lead, in turn, to the finalization of an additional tendency of the old liberals, the reduction of theology to ethics. Toward the middle of his discussion, van Buren indicates that the linguistic philosophers with whom he has cast his lot have demonstrated with force and clarity the unity of ethics and

theology intrinsic to theological language.[31] Toward the end of the
book, he admits the reduction of theology to ethics and defends it in
the name of modern secular thought.[32] The analysis of the secular
meaning of the gospel that lies between these two comments illustrates what he is talking about. When we deal with the Easter event
of the gospel, van Buren says, we are not dealing with an account
of or a faith in a physical resurrection of Jesus of Nazareth on which
we build the hope of our own resurrection. Rather, what the New
Testament tells us about Easter is that this is the day when Jesus'
freedom to be a "man for others" became contagious for the disciples.
The Easter kerygma is a perspective on Jesus' history and on human
existence in history generally.[33] Given this perspective of freedom for
others as the central meaning of the Easter gospel, New Testament
Christology and theology are dissolved into an ethical anthropology:
"We would emphasize, along with many contemporary interpretations
of Christology, that the Christian perspective sees the 'true nature' of
man in precisely the freedom for the others which was Jesus' own.
Human being is being free for one's neighbor."[34] The "eschatological
hope" of the believer who has been grasped by this perspective of
freedom for others lies in his conviction that this freedom will enable
reconciliation among men to prevail on earth.[35]

Van Buren has been criticized from a variety of angles, not the
least of which is the criticism taking him on his own terms and demonstrating the difficulties and limitations of the "logic" of his logical
positivism.[36] Much of what I have already said in connection with
Schleiermacher and Ritschl would also go for van Buren—only more
so. Perhaps one of the most interesting criticisms, however, is that
offered by Carl Braaten. It ties in with the previous observation that
for van Buren eschatology is understood solely in terms of a moral
commitment to reconciliation among men. As a "death of God"
theology, Braaten considers van Buren's theology to be "futureless."
As such, in the absence of God who, as the power of the future,
brings in the future kingdom of his promise, there is no hope.[37] In
"forsaking God for the sake of man," van Buren has substituted
for the "end-words" of Jesus' eschatology the "ought-words" of ethics.
"It is true enough," says Braaten, "that we can get to the ethics of
Jesus only by way of his eschatology, but the eschatology is not so
much scaffolding that can be discarded once we reach the ethics."[38]

The eschatology of classical Christian theology may have tended toward dichotomizing man and disparaging concern for nature and history, but van Buren's notions eliminate eschatology altogether and steal from us a meaningful future within which to understand our present. This is not only a betrayal of the Christian faith of all ages; it is not even sufficiently responsive to the modern view of reality, dominated as it is by the lure of the future.[39]

Unlike van Buren, Harvey Cox does not believe that God is dead nor does he believe that speaking of God is an insurmountable linguistic problem in the twentieth century. Indeed, Cox maintains that Christianity must speak of God. However, when we do, we need to be aware that we are "naming" something that we confess and locate in our historical experience. Naming is not defining or describing—that would be speaking *about* God. Speaking about God is the way of the theistic metaphysics of the past, and a metaphysically mediated outlook on reality is incompatible with our secular epoch. To speak of God in a secular fashion for our time is to name him in terms appropriate to our secularized view of things. This involves seeing the matter as a sociological problem, a political issue, and a theological question.[40]

As a sociological problem, speaking of God in a secular fashion is simply a matter of divesting ourselves of the religious and metaphysical trappings of traditional God-talk which deny us access to a world dominated by the secular spirit. As a political issue, speaking of God in a secular fashion means recognizing that the political idiom is the appropriate successor to the metaphysical in addressing the urban-secular consciousness. The political realm does what metaphysics had done in the past by bringing unity and meaning to human life and thought. Taking Paul Lehman's lead, Cox maintains that a secular theology that speaks of God politically is one that discerns what God is doing in the concrete activities of history and then joins him. In acting politically for the humanization of the world one speaks of God in a secular fashion. Finally, as a theological concern, secular God-talk begins with the recognition that God does not "appear" but is the free and hidden God who shows man that he acts in history and invites man to realize his humanity in cooperative response to that action. God is not man nor is he another way of speaking about man. He *is* the wholly other to whom we respond. However, our response is not in terms of I-Thou encounter, which Cox ascribes to the era of town culture and individualism when God was seen as the one who appears to us as the authority *over* us. Rather, our response in the age of the secular city is one based on an I-You partnership relationship with God in which we cooperate with God in the processes of history for the realization of the future he intends. As yet, Cox has no proposal for the new names and words of secular theology. That will come, he says, when God is ready. Conceptualizing God is something that emerges out of human culture and history in terms of what man experiences of what we call God. In the process of cooperative response within urban civilization the name of God will become apparent.[41]

Cox's program for speaking of God in a secular fashion is not simply an accommodation to his perception of the modern consciousness. Throughout his theology Cox accords a certain normative function to the biblical witness as he understands it. He maintains the popular thesis that biblical faith is the authentic source of secularization in Western culture. Secularization is a liberating phenomenon in which man "comes of age," and takes possession of and responsibility for a world and history that have been relativized by deliverance from the fatalistic domination of mythical supernatural forces. A prime example of how the biblical outlook on reality has been a major influence on the development of secular consciousness is, of course, the doctrine of creation. In the Bible God is separated from nature as its Creator and man is distinguished from nature in his special role of domination and care for the creation. The natural world is desacralized and the way is paved for the free utilization and manipulation of its resources in the development of science and technology.[42] According to Cox, the biblical outlook achieves a similar desacralization of the world in the realms of value and politics as well.

From the perspective of his conviction that the roots of secularization can be found in biblical faith, it is easy to see, as we have just observed, how Cox can settle for a theology mediated by the language of political action instead of one that is under the sway of myth or metaphysics. This is evident also in his eschatology. The kingdom of God is interpreted by Cox as something that is neither in the future nor already realized. Rather, it is in the process of realization. The secular city is the concrete manifestation of the symbol of the kingdom. Man is called to partnership with God in taking responsibility for the shaping and directing of the secular city in opposition to the dehumanizing forces of our times.[43] Christ has won the victory over these forces, and we are called to realize continually the concrete fruits of that victory throughout the processes of history.

> Exodus and Easter remain the two foci of biblical faith, the basis on which a theology of the church must be developed. The Exodus is the event which sets forth "what God is doing in history." He is seen to be liberating people from bondage, releasing them from political, cultural, and economic captivity, providing them with the occasion to forge in the wilderness a new symbol system, a new set of values, and a new national identity. Easter means that the same activity goes on today, and that where such liberating activity occurs, the same Yahweh of Hosts is at work. Both Exodus and Easter are caught up in the inclusive symbol of the Kingdom, the realization of the liberating rule of God. In our terms, God's action today, through secularization and urbanization, puts man in an unavoidable crisis. He must take responsibility in and for the city of man or become once again a slave to dehumanizing powers.[44]

In his theology of the kingdom of God, Cox takes pains to distinguish his view from that of the old social gospel movement. He notes that this movement was indeed marred by the mistaken notion that the kingdom is somehow man's work. Moreover, the social gospel version of the kingdom became fused with equally problematic ideas about progress and social betterment.[45]

However, it seems fair to question the extent to which Cox has really disabused himself of these social gospel characteristics. He may insist that the kingdom is God's work but his rather Pelagian concept of man's partnership with God in shaping the secular city takes the edge off this insistence. Furthermore, as Roger Shinn has observed, Harvey Cox ". . . although he does not go so far as to reinstate the old doctrine of progress, comes close to it. He finds the processes of secularization to be inevitable and irreversible. And secularization is very close to progress."[46] As we have seen, secularization liberates man for maturity in taking responsibility for the future of his world. Such liberation is a decidedly hopeful and humanizing thing in Cox's view. Thus, although Harvey Cox maintains the distinction between God and man as an important premise in his theology, his Pelagian tendencies together with the relativistic, secularized character of his eschatology finally serve to concentrate our focus on man's perception of God's activity in history and man's responsible action in history as a response to that perception. Consequently, the man-centered, history-centered characteristics of nineteenth century liberal theology reemerge here couched in the new terminology of urban secularity.

Rudolf Bultmann's views, when compared with the other modes of secularizing thought we have reviewed, display both similarities and differences. Bultmann's program of demythologizing is well known. It requires little discussion here except for reminding ourselves of some of the basic ingredients of his manifesto, "New Testament and Mythology." Bultmann believes that the New Testament world view is thoroughly immersed in the mythology of its prescientific age. In our contemporary world, shaped as it is by modern science, the mythical world of the New Testament is obsolete.[47] Succinctly put, Bultmann states that "it is impossible to use the electric light and the wireless and to avail ourselves of modern medical and surgical discoveries, and at the same time to believe in the New Testament world of spirits and miracles."[48] It is for this reason that demythologizing must be practiced as a consistent interpretation of this mythological framework for the purpose of laying bare the real message of the kerygma. To fail to do so will render the proclamation of the New Testament unintelligible and will obscure the true message it imports. Bultmann's assertion of the need to demythologize as both an insight of modern thought and a response to modern thought is evidence of a measure of continuity with his liberal antecedents and with contemporary secularizers. However, the further development of his response to the modern scientific world view is distinctive.

For Bultmann the essential purpose of New Testament mythology is to present us with the possibility and challenge of authentic existence. This determination reflects, of course, Bultman's marriage with existential philosophy, especially the thought of Martin Heidegger.[49] One offspring of that bond is a decidedly different attitude toward history and eschatology from that of the old liberals and certain modern secularizers like Harvey Cox. Bultmann acknowledges with Weiss and Schweitzer that the central proclamation of Jesus was the kingdom of God as an imminent eschatological hope. However, history has refuted this mythologically framed expectation, and the work of Weiss has refuted the progressivist interpretation of the kingdom by the Ritschlian school and the social gospel movement.[50] Both of these refuted interpretations of the kingdom relate it to universal history. Bultmann proposes instead that we offer an existential interpretation which relates the proclamation of the kingdom to the personal history of the individual. By this interpretation the real message of the kerygma is that God in Jesus Christ enables us to be open to his future which is imminent for each individual.[51] To be open to God's future for our lives is to be freed from all man-made securities for the life of faith and love. Eschatological existence is a possibility now. "God has acted, and the world—'this world'—has come to an end. Man himself has been made new."[52]

An individualized and realized eschatology such as Bultmann proposes accords with Heidegger's view of history as primarily concerned with the personal history of individuals in their confrontation with the possibility of authentic or inauthentic existence. Heidegger is interested in neither the scientific study of history nor the universal meaning of history. Rather, history is to disclose to us the authentic possibilities of man that are "repeatable"—possibilities that were once open to the human *Dasein* in a past situation and are retrievable for the future of our personal present.[53] The eschatological event of Jesus of Nazareth is the possibility of authentic human existence *par excellence* that may be continually retrieved through the proclamation of the kerygma for the personal history of all people.[54] Thus, the man-centeredness and history-centeredness of secularizing thought that we have traced to this point are apparent also in Bultmann. However, in his existential interpretation of the New Testament the two foci become one. The center of man is his personal history and the center of history is the personal history of man.

By shifting the focus of eschatology from the meaning of or end of universal history to man's individual historicity, Bultmann has dehistoricized eschatology and de-eschatologized history. The eschatological moment occurs for you and me when, confronted by the authentic existence revealed in Jesus, we *decide* to understand the meaning of our personal history in terms of this possibility. In doing so we *obey* God by letting his future be our future. Thus, in his Gifford Lectures, Bultmann concludes:

. . . the meaning in history always lies in the present, and when the present is conceived as the eschatological present by Christian faith the meaning in history is realized. Man who complains: "I cannot see meaning in history, and therefore my life, interwoven in history, is meaningless," is to be admonished: do not look around yourself into universal history, you must look into your own personal history. Always in your present lies the meaning of history, and you cannot see it as a spectator, but only in your responsible decisions. In every moment slumbers the possibility of being the eschatological moment. You must awaken it.[55]

This important capsule of Bultmann's outlook not only illustrates the distinctiveness of his perspective on history and eschatology; it also shows that the outcome of his thought is a tendency for theology to collapse into ethics. In this he is close to the other secular thinkers we have been discussing. Indeed, it is basic to Bultmann's understanding of the New Testament that Jesus' eschatological message and his ethical message constitute a unity.[56] In fairness to Bultmann, he does maintain that authentic eschatological existence is a function of faith which is by grace and not by works. However, statements like the previous quotation from the Gifford Lectures and his consistent emphasis on decision and obedience as part of the structure of faith leave one questioning whether or not the distinction between grace and works is actually somewhat blurred.

In the final analysis, Bultmann's theology reveals an element of genuine irony. He begins his program of demythologizing with the premise that the mythical, prescientific world view of the New Testament is obsolete for modern scientific man. Consequently, it must be interpreted in terms of its true purpose which is to confront us with a possibility of authentic existence. However, the existential interpretation of the kerygma abandons the secular world to whomever wants it. As Christians we are called upon to understand the significance of the gospel as restricted to the personal history of individuals. Thus, we have a dualism between spiritual life and worldly life that is every bit as radical as the dualism we encounter in certain forms of myth and in certain developments of the Christian tradition—dualisms which the other representatives of secular theology have sought to overcome in various ways. It is, therefore, doubtful that Bultmann's reading of the New Testament makes the scandal of the kerygma more accessible to the modern secular consciousness.

CONCLUSION

Throughout this chapter it has been my intention to characterize "secularized man." What has actually transpired is a more general discussion of the secular outlook, as expressed in the old liberalism and the new secularism. However, the common features of the various thinkers do in fact indicate a view of man that is decidedly secularized. In contrast to the dichotomized man of the past, the secular outlook sees man's nature and destiny in thoroughly historical terms. In view of this, man's religious nature tends to find its authentic expression in striving at the ethical task rather than in seeking an other-worldly salvation and fulfillment.

I have been critical along the way. However, it must be noted that the secular outlook represents a sincere attempt to deal with the troublesome problems of understanding God's relationship to his world in a scientific era where the dualisms of the past are unacceptable. In this attempt certain real benefits have been reaped for contemporary theology. The secularizing of theology and of its understanding of man has restored history to a place of importance. It has underscored the need to affirm this world and to take responsibility for it. Furthermore, the secular theologians have recovered eschatology as a central theme of Christian theology and have demonstrated its vital connection with the Christian ethic. This is an important accomplishment to which I shall refer as the discussion progresses.

However, the fundamental criticism of secularizing thought must stand. It is, I believe, fair to say that those treated in this chapter would all in some measure fall under Paul Tillich's criticism of autonomy. Autonomy as an interpretation of reality places man and his history in the center of reality. In so doing, it is guilty of the profanation of reality by eroding our awareness and appreciation of the transcendent which is the ground of all that exists. Tillich offers instead the notion of theonomy. The theonomous outlook is the subject of our next chapter.

Chapter IV

Theonomous Man

As I have already indicated in the introductory first chapter, the idea of a theonomous understanding of man in the image of God has its roots in Augustine and its modern expression in the work of Paul Tillich, who has made the concept of theonomy famous. The theonomous outlook sees the image of God as referring to the special way in which man's whole being is constituted by an ontological communion with the divine. For this reason one might well describe this view as "ontological monism." It is monistic in two senses. First of all, neither Augustine nor Tillich divides the image in the fashion we observed among those who have a twofold doctrine of the image. The image of God is seen as a single, comprehensive phenomenon. Secondly, both Augustine and Tillich avoid explicit and implicit dualism by not restricting the significance of the image for the being and destiny of man to the soul or the spirit as opposed to man's bodily and historical existence. The Neoplatonic tendencies of both Augustine and Tillich may appear at times to make this last assertion a hazardous one. Moreover, the eschatological viewpoint of both thinkers forces one to question how effectively they actually avoid the sort of dualism that divides the being of man in terms of eternal destiny versus historical existence. Were such a dualism to triumph in their thought they would verge on seeing man from a heteronomous point of view. That is, the fulfillment of the *humanum* would ultimately be understood as coming in a mode of existence other than or discontinuous with (*heteros*) natural, historical human existence. However, although there may be inconsistencies in the thought of both men, their mutual stress on the immediate and integral relationship between the being of God and the being of man secures their designation as exponents of "theonomous man."

SAINT AUGUSTINE

At first glance, Augustine's doctrine of the image of God appears simply to identify the image with reason as the peculiar characteristic that sets man above the animals. In *The Trinity,* our richest source for this doctrine, Augustine states:

> Our design for preparing the reader, by the study of the things that are made, for the knowledge of their maker has brought us to the image of God which man presents, in virtue of that which sets him above all other animals: namely, reason or intelligence, with any other characteristic of the reasonable or intellectual soul that is properly to be assigned to what we call *mens* or *animus* (mind).[1]

This description of the image in rational terms is echoed throughout the treatise. Indeed, Augustine appears to go even further toward a rationalistic definition of the image in his discussion of Eph. 4:23 and Col. 3:9, 10. These passages deal with the renewal of the Christian in the image of God as constituting a renewal of mind and knowledge. They prompt the following remarks:

> If then we are renewed in the spirit of our mind, and he is the new man who is renewed to the knowledge of God after the image of Him that created him; no one can doubt that man was made after the image of Him that created him, not according to the body, nor indiscriminately according to any part of the mind, but according to the rational mind, wherein the knowledge of God can exist.[2]

However, this evidence notwithstanding, it is clear elsewhere in Augustine's writings that Reinhold Neibuhr is correct in saying that he means more by the rational soul or intellect of man than simply the capacity for discursive reasoning. Rather, the rational or intellectual soul of man is immortal, abiding, and indelible; in it the image of its Creator is "planted immortally." The rational soul is, thus, the abiding feature of man's being whereby he is able to apprehend God.[3]

For Niebuhr this view of the rational soul is an instance of Augustine's Neoplatonic heritage coming to the aid of his biblical faith. Augustine, claims Niebuhr, is interested here and elsewhere in the human spirit's capacity for self-transcendence. As a Neoplatonist, Augustine sought God in the mystery of self-consciousness. In so doing, he took as his point of departure a common ground shared by mysticism and Christianity, "the understanding that the human spirit in its depth and height reaches into eternity and that this vertical dimension is more important for the understanding of man than merely his rational capacity for forming general concepts."[4]

Paul Tillich states the matter even more profoundly. He sees the influence of Neoplatonism as the source for Augustine's understanding of the relationship between God and the world. Augustine believed that "God is the creative ground of the world in terms of *amor* (love)" and that there is, therefore, an immediate experience of the divine in everything, especially the soul. This is why Augustine wants to know the soul. Only there can one know God. God, perceived in the soul, is not an object among other objects. He is the center of man's being and the *a priori* of man's being. In the soul's immediate knowledge of God there is no split between subject and object wherein man the subject knows God as an object. This gap is overcome because "God is given to the subject as nearer to itself than it is to itself."[5]

Emil Brunner's interpretation adds to this picture. He points out that Augustine introduced a new idea of the image that broke down the dual scheme of Irenaeus. With regard to Augustine's attempts in *The Trinity* to find the image of the Trinity in the being of man, Brunner observes that the threefold psychological functions of man are not themselves the image of the Trinity. Augustine's point is that these threefold structures in the human spirit serve as the basis for man to be reminded of God, to understand him, and to love him. Given this immediacy of God to the being of man in the image of God, it is understandable that Augustine can consider it rightful self-love when the spirit loves God through whom the image is created and renewed. Though colored by Neoplatonism, Augustine's discussion of the image has for Brunner captured the central truth, "that man's being as a whole, both original and fallen, should be understood from the point of view of the being-in-the-Word-of-God."[6]

Naturally, Niebuhr, Tillich, and Brunner tend to read Augustine in such a way that his thoughts come out very close to their own. However, their combined witness presents a clear consensus that for Augustine the image of God in man represents the fact that man's being is determined by an immediate ontological relationship to God. Man's ability in his rational soul to know and love God is both the evidence of this relationship and the result of this relationship. This reading is supported not only by scattered statements from *The Trinity* but by the presupposition of the work itself. The fact that man is created in the image of God is, for Augustine, the basis of his efforts to seek analogies to the Trinity in the threefold psychological functions of the human spirit. By looking into the depths of his own being, man can discern the impress of God. Augustine's discussions of the mystical journey of the soul toward God provide further evidence of this understanding. The first step of the journey is that of the soul toward itself for the return to oneself is a stepping stone to God:

> Recognize in yourself something within, within yourself. Leave abroad both your clothing and your flesh; descend into yourself; go to your secret chamber, your mind. If you are far from your own self, how can you draw near to God. . . . the initial stage discloses the motive and goal of the entire journey. The life of devotion is a quest for the truth which has first of all to be sought in the inward parts. There is truth in man which is the imaged reflection of God.[7]

As this self-seeking becomes self-knowledge, the second stage is reached. "The 'soul in itself' is the spirit's own consciousness that it is made in God's image. To be so made means that the spirit is capable of receiving and comprehending God's own truth, mirrored truly though never completely within man's own self."[8]

These ideas have been disparagingly labeled as Augustine's revision of the Platonic theory of recollection but Augustine himself believed them to be grounded in Scripture.[9] And Niebuhr has pointed out that Augustine's biblical faith and his emphasis on the need for special revelation ultimately preserve him from any deification of the self-consciousness. For Augustine faith is the presupposition of understanding. Man's powers point to God but they cannot fully comprehend him.[10] Indeed, in *The Trinity* Augustine is explicit about the limitations and inadequacies of the image of God in man. Man is not fully the image of God. He is only *after* the image. He is not equal by parity with God but shares in a likeness. Consequently, every analogy with man's spirit which is developed in the work is ultimately unsatisfactory for it can only hint at a truth it does not actually embody. Furthermore, by his own fault man has in sin changed for the worse what likeness he does possess. "Hence," says Augustine, "we can never rise to the knowledge of God as he actually is. We can only get hints and intimations, as we ascend from the world of the senses to those higher aspects of man's being which more nearly reflect the divine."[11]

Clearly Augustine does not employ the sort of twofold interpretation of the image we found in Irenaeus and Aquinas and, in vestigial form, in Luther as well. Consequently, there is no "structural dualism" in his anthropology. Moreover, his sense of the ontological communion between God and man whereby the rational soul has an immediate intimation of the divine precludes specifically the sort of dichotomy between natural and supranatural or reason and revelation that is so characteristic of Thomistic thought.

Paul Tillich has contrasted the approach to the knowledge of God in Augustine and Aquinas in terms of "The Augustinian Solution" and "The Thomistic Dissolution." Tillich's point is that for Augustine and those who developed his thought in the thirteenth century (Alexander of Hales, Bonaventura, and Matthew of Aquasparta) God and Being coincide in the nature of Truth. This fundamental coincidence of the two Ultimates, *Deus* and *Esse,* constitutes the Augustinian solution:

> The question of the two Ultimates is solved in such a way that the religious Ultimate is presupposed in every philosophical question, including the question of God. *God is the presupposition of the question of God*: This is the ontological solution of the problem of the philosophy of religion. God can never be reached if he is the *object* of a question, and not its basis.[12]

As a result of this ontological solution, Augustine and his followers were able to say that God is knowable without mediation and with a certainty that is as certain as Being itself.[13] In the Thomistic dissolution, the cosmological approach to the knowledge of God renders God as the object of the question, a particular being rather than Being itself. Human reason pursuing the cosmological arguments for the existence of God can only demonstrate the rational probability of God's existence; real knowledge of God comes by the authority of special revelation. God and Being are separated; the former becomes a singular being of overwhelming power and the latter is formalized in terms of a philosophical explanation of the structures of finite nature.[14] In this scheme of thought the dichotomy between natural and supranatural and reason and revelation is solidified.

The Thomistic dissolution, as Tillich terms it, is clearly what he would also call a heteronomous outlook on reality; ultimate truth is imposed from outside by authority. Inasmuch as the Thomistic view of man divides him in terms of a natural and supranatural image, the latter elevated above the former, we have a dichotomy which is the corollary of the disjunction between reason and revelation. Put another way, in Thomas we have a heteronomous view of man. By contrast the ontological approach to the knowledge of God, the Augustinian solution, would qualify as a theonomous outlook on reality, given the fact that in a theonomous view all reality is grounded in and transparent to the Ground of All Being which is God or Being-itself. Augustine's view of man in the image as a rational soul with unmediated apprehension of the divine as closer to the self than the self is to itself represents a theonomous understanding of man corresponding to his general ontological approach to the question of God.

Augustine's monism stands in contrast to the tradition of twofold concepts of the image, and his theonomous "solution" stands in contrast to the duality of the Thomistic dissolution. However, is it not fair to say that Augustine's emphasis on the image as the *rational soul* betrays a hint of spirit-matter dualism due to the influence of Neoplatonism? I believe that this tendency is mitigated, at least to some extent, by certain remarks Augustine makes in connection with the effects of sin on the image and the hope we have for salvation from that sin. In speaking of the Fall of man from his primitive state, Augustine makes clear that the undefiled image prior to the Fall is attended by a state of perfection in which man's entire being is whole. Consequently, Augustine's description of the effects of the Fall enumerates those that corrupt both body and spirit: death, depravity, lust, and so forth. Had the Fall not occurred, had the image not been defaced by man's misuse of his free will, man's whole being would still possess the "wholeness" intended by the Creator.[15] Correspondingly, the hope we have in Christ is in the promise of the resurrection to a spiritual body in which spirit and flesh will be in harmony and the body cleansed of all its corruption.[16] This, we may presume, is a concomitant of the renewal of the image by grace in Christ. Therefore, despite the flavor of Neoplatonism in Augustine's thought, he is ultimately preserved from a thoroughgoing Greek dualism by his biblical faith.

Nonetheless, when we consider closely this last discussion of what is lost in the Fall and what is restored in the resurrection, we are led to question whether or not Augustine expresses what I have previously referred to as a dualism which proceeds from an ahistorical eschatology. Augustine does speak of a total loss of the image and he does not think in terms of a loss of that part of the image which represents original righteousness (the divine *similitudo* in Irenaeus and the supernatural image in Aquinas). As we have seen, he considers the image to be an expression of our abiding ontological communion with God. Although the harmony and integrity of this communion are marred by sin, the essential relationship remains nonetheless. Consequently, we cannot expect his eschatology to present a clear-cut return-to-origins motif in which what is lost in the beginning is simply restored in the end. Still, because he does believe that there was an actual primitive state of perfection, in paradise from which man has fallen, the stage is set for a modified form of restoration eschatology.

Several things are clear from Augustine's discussion of the paradise condition in his monumental work *The City of God*. First of all, while he allows that an allegorical interpretation of the Genesis account of paradise and Fall can capture the spirit of its message, he still insists on its historicity. Secondly, it is also clear that he teaches something like an original righteousness prior to the Fall; he contends that, had our first parents not sinned, they would have remained immortal. The resurrection in the life of the world to come will therefore bring a renewal of the lost perfection of paradise, though not a simple return to that state, for the spiritual body of the resurrection will in certain respects represent a higher perfection.[17] When he refers this hope of the end to the image of God specifically, we find that it includes man's being formed again in the image which was deformed by the Fall.[18] According to Emil Brunner's analysis, Augustine established here for the first time the notion of the primitive state of integrity. It has been normative for the tradition ever since. It is the existence of this teaching, in Brunner's estimate, which accounts in large measure for the development of dualistic concepts of man by making it inevitable that we think in dichotomous terms about what man is, viewed from his origins, and what he is, viewed from his historical existence.[19]

Ernst Benz further explicates the dualistic tendencies of Augustine's eschatology. Benz has demonstrated that with Augustine the lively hope in the early church for an immediate arrival of the kingdom of God came to a formal end. Augustine offered an "ecclesiastical positivism" which identified the visible catholic church with the kingdom of God as a substitute for the hope of its early eschatological arrival. In this way he de-eschatologized the doctrine of the kingdom and laid the foundations for the monolithic authority of the visible catholic church and its hierarchy. This equation of membership in the kingdom of God with membership in the church on earth introduced a strong element of realized eschatology into the tradition of Christian thought. As a consequence, the significance of the promise and expectation of the universal eschatological kingdom for the Christian's understanding of the meaning of self and history recedes into the background. Indeed, Augustine taught a doctrine of two resurrections whereby the idea of membership in the church as membership in the heavenly kingdom of God on earth is strengthened in the proposition that the first resurrection, which is of the Spirit, is sealed already in baptism.[20]

The conrast between the church as the eternal kingdom of God on earth and the earthly kingdom of historical existence is given formal expression in the contrast between the City of God and the City of Earth. Augustine placed the destinies of the two cities outside one another. In so doing, "he laid the foundation for both a church-centeredness and dualism that cuts the veins that run from the kingdom of God through the body of this world."[21] The cumulative effect of Augustine's eschatology, then, is to produce a dualism in our understanding of man which pits his spiritual and suprahistorical nature as a member of the City of God against his historical nature as a member of the City of Earth. The ultimate outcome of this scheme for the Christian attitude toward participation in the world leads, on the one hand, to the kind of hierarchical conservatism witnessed in the Thomistic system and, on the other hand, to the bifurcation of the two kingdoms doctrine of the Lutheran tradition.[22] Thus, in the final analysis, Augustine's ahistorical eschatology led him to an heteronomous outlook on history and human destiny that offset to some extent his achievement of a theonomous view of human nature.

PAUL TILLICH

As should be obvious by now, Paul Tillich readily identifies with the theological tradition of St. Augustine. Tillich's additional comments make this identification specific:

> In the Augustinian tradition the source of all philosophy of religion is the immediacy of the presence of God in the soul or, as I prefer to say it, the experience of the unconditional, of the ultimate, in terms of an ultimate or unconditional concern. This is the *prius* of everything.[23]

> I would say, almost unambiguously, that I myself, and my whole theology, stand much more in the line of the Augustinian than in the Thomistic tradition . . . a philosophy of religion which is based on the immediacy of the truth in every human being.[24]

As a concomitant of these statements, Tillich also finds a common ground with Augustine in their respective doctrines of God. According to Tillich, Augustine taught:

> The world is created in every moment by the divine will, which is the will of love. Therefore, Augustine concluded—and the Reformers followed him—that the creation and preservation are the same thing; the world is at no moment independent of God. . . . God is the supporting power of being, which has the character of love. This makes every deistic fixation of the two realities—God and the world—impossible. God is the continuous, carrying ground of the world.[25]

It is this vision of God as "the continuous, carrying ground of the world" (Tillich, *The Ground of All Being*) that makes it possible for Augustine and Tillich to speak of "the immediacy of the truth in every human being." And it is, perhaps, these statements concerning Tillich's identification of himself with the Augustinian tradition that provide us with some of the best clues to understanding his direct statements concerning man in the image of God.

In his *Systematic Theology* Tillich begins his brief discussion of the *imago Dei* by rejecting the dualistic doctrine of the Roman Catholic tradition, which Tillich believes follows Irenaeus's distinction between *imago and similitudo*. The former refers to the natural equipment of man, that which distinguishes him from the rest of creation, and the latter is a *donum superadditum,* which enabled Adam to adhere to God. Protestantism, Tillich points out, refused to accept this dichotomy between nature and grace or nature and supernature and, therefore, abandoned the distinction between *imago* and *similitudo* as well. Protestantism stressed the *justitia originalis* based on man's power for communion and union with God. With the Fall this communion and righteousness are lost and there is no remaining freedom for return. In the Roman tradition some freedom remains to man by which he might again turn to God because what was lost in the Fall was something outside man's being proper, the *donum superadditum.*

For Tillich the choice between the two traditions is not a totally satisfactory choice. His critique on ontological supernaturalism makes it evident that he could not live with the Catholic position.[26] However, he does not regard the Protestant solution as wholly adequate either. The Protestant understanding of the image as a reference to the original righteousness of perfect communion with God is not without its liabilities. While the image of God is the condition which makes communion with God possible, it is not legitimate to define the image as that *communion* itself. Rather, man is the image of God in terms of that which distinguishes him from all other creatures, his rational structure.[27]

As was the case with Augustine's "rational soul," so also here, Tillich means more by man's "rational structure" or reason than simply his intellectual powers. For Tillich,

> . . . reason is the structure of freedom, and it implies potential infinity. Man is the image of God because in him the ontological elements are complete and united on a creaturely basis, just as they are complete and united in God as the creative ground. Man is the image of God because his *logos* is analogous to the divine *logos,* so that the divine *logos* can appear as man without destroying the humanity of man.[28]

Thus, Tillich defines the precise nature of the image in terms of man's ontological structure as grounded in and reflecting the ontological structure of God who is Being itself. Although man's being is derivative and the ontological elements are limited by the marks of his finitude, he still shares in the *logos* structure of God. As with Augustine, so also with Tillich, the image of God signals an ontological communion with God. Consequently, Tillich can further echo Augustine when he states in his own terms that, by sharing in the *logos* structure of the divine, man experiences the immediacy of the presence of God or of the ultimate.

This conception of the image of God is further elucidated by Tillich under the rubric of man's "freedom" and his "centeredness." In that man possesses analogically the ontological elements which are united in God, he possesses freedom. However, the potentialities of man's freedom are limited by what Tillich terms the pole of destiny. Man's freedom is finite freedom. Nonetheless, human freedom is man's greatness over against the rest of the created world. It is symbolized by the "image of God." However, at the same time, freedom is the source of man's weakness for it is that aspect of man's being that makes the Fall possible. Only because man possesses freedom can he separate himself from God. Without such freedom man would not have personal existence as we normally understand the idea of the personal; he would be reduced to a thing.[29] It appears, then, that the image of God, indicating ontological communion with God, refers, as such, to human *personhood* or *selfhood*, expressed in freedom—a freedom which is perceived in the *logos* structure which man shares with the divine *logos*.

That the image for Tillich indicates selfhood becomes even more apparent in his discussion of human centeredness. Centeredness is a concomitant of freedom and, like freedom, it is the source of both man's greatness and his weakness. Man's greatness and dignity as the image of God refer to the fact that he is the only creature with self-consciousness and, therefore, the only completely centered being. This complete centeredness "indicates his ability to transcend both himself and his world, to look at both, and to converge."[30] In being a self and having a world, man is the perfection of creation. But this perfection is at the same time man's temptation. The temptation is to leave his essential center in the divine ground and regard himself as the center of himself and his world. In the freedom of his centeredness man feels he has the capacity to do this even though he recognizes the finitude of his freedom. This is precisely what has taken place in *estrangement*, which is Tillich's word for the state of fallen man. "In estrangement, man is outside the divine center to which his own center essentially belongs."[31] Thus, man's ability in freedom and centeredness to step outside the divine center and choose to be the center of his own existence is both the measure of his dignity as an autonomous self and the occasion of his tragic estrangement from God.

In *Dynamics of Faith* all three of the ways in which Tillich speaks of the *imago Dei*—immediacy of awareness of God in ontological communion, freedom, and centeredness—are brought together as elements of a unified concept of the person. Faith, says Tillich, is an act of the centered personality; it is an act of the total man, bringing into play all the elements of man's makeup: reason, emotion, will. As such, faith is a function of freedom for freedom is essentially the possibility of centered acts. Faith is therefore the quintessentially personal act because it brings together all elements of man's being in an experience of the "ecstatic" which transcends the drives of all the structures of man's nature—rational and nonrational—without destroying them. However, this faith, this act of being grasped by the divine, rests upon the potential of the self to have an immediate understanding and awareness of the infinite. We are thus driven back to the initial observation that there is an element of infinity in man; he shares analogically in the ontological structure of the divine.[32]

> Man is able to understand in an immediate personal and central act the meaning of the ultimate, the unconditional, the absolute, the infinite. This alone makes faith a human potentiality.
> Human potentialities are powers that drive toward actualization. Man is driven toward faith by his awareness of the infinite to which he belongs, but which he does not own like a possession. This is in abstract terms what concretely appears as the "restlessness of the heart within the flux of life."[33]

Tillich's concept of man in the image of God is thoroughly monistic. The image refers to human personhood as the phenomenon in which all the elements of man's being are seen as united in the centered self as grounded in and reflective of the divine ground of all being.

Obviously, what we have in Tillich's view of man in the image of God is a theonomous understanding of man. This accords with Tillich's theonomous approach to the questions of Christian social ethics which are a facet of the larger question of the relationship between religion and culture. Tillich pursued these matters under the rubric of the kingdom of God. The kingdom of God stands beyond the contrast of autonomy and heteronomy. The indication of its nearness at any moment in history—albeit in penultimate form—is in the achievement of theonomy, the unitive overcoming of the contrast between autonomy (culture) and heteronomy (religion).[34] "Theonomy asserts that the superior law is, at the same time, the

innermost law of man himself, rooted in the divine ground which
is man's own ground: the law of life transcends man although it is at
the same time his own."[35] Therefore, in a theonomous culture, "Religion is the substance of culture and culture the form of religion."[36]

Theonomy, as the impact of the Spiritual Presence, recalls secularizing culture from its profane self-reliance and religion from its
demonic exclusiveness of regarding itself as the sole repository of the
holy. When such a theonomous situation develops in history, there
is a creative unification of the truth of heteronomy and the truth of
autonomy, and this constitutes a drawing near of the kingdom of
God. Energized by this vision, Tillich became passionately involved in
the cause of religious socialism in prewar Germany. He regarded the
prospect of a theonomous union of Christianity and socialism to be
a new cultural and political breakthrough of the kingdom of God.[37]

However, in the final analysis, Tillich's theology is not wholly
adequate to the problem of the church and the world. The kingdom
of God in Tillich's thought is not ultimately an historical concept.
Its fulfillment is above history in eternal life. In terms of our historical
existence, the kingdom is "always and never," an endless series of
fragmentary attainments of theonomy rather than a hoped-for
ultimate fulfillment of world history: "The end of historical time is its
relation to the ultimate. Thus, the ultimate stands equally close to
and equally distant from each moment in history."[38] These thoughts
stand in contrast to Tillich's more historical understanding of the
kingdom of God, and this contrast constitutes a continual tension
in Tillich's work. Indeed, in the very same article just quoted,
Tillich rejects the Greek depreciation of time and the general idea
of the eternal return of all things. Elsewhere he states that to choose
Christianity is to choose the historical interpretation of history as
represented by Greek thought.[39]

In the end, in Tillich's eschatology, it seems to me that the tension
in his thought is resolved more along Platonic lines than in terms of
the Judeo-Christian emphasis on the historical. The kingdom of God
is not the ultimate, eschatological fulfillment of history foreshadowed
by penultimate historical manifestations of theonomy. The future
eschaton of history is swallowed up in the permanent presence of
eternal life.[40] Eternal life, as contrasted with historical existence, is the
focus of our hope for human fulfillment, not the redemption of his-

tory. This is clear from Tillich's doctrine of "essentialization" which is a revision of Origen's idea of the *apocatastasis panton*, the restitution of everything in eternity.[41] Notwithstanding the fact that Tillich's monistic anthropology overcomes Origen's spirit-matter dualism,[42] the dualism of eternity versus history remains. Consequently, man's being is once more divided despite the brilliance of Tillich's theonomous doctrine of man as the image of God. So he writes in the final chapter of his *Systematic Theology*, "everything temporal comes from the eternal and returns to the eternal."[43]

TRANSITIONAL COMMENTS

I think it helpful at this point to recapitulate briefly. The overall task of this study is to demonstrate the contributions that eschatological theology can make to a contemporary understanding of man and the significance of that understanding for the explication of the Christian ethic. I noted at the outset that the Christian ethic of love requires a clear understanding of the human good or of the human fulfillment toward which love strives. However, we are forced to acknowledge immediately that the tradition of Christian anthropology up to the present has left us with a lack of consensus regarding the nature and fulfillment of human existence. The mixed witness of the tradition does not indicate that the church has somehow failed in understanding man from the Christian perspective. Rather, what it illustrates is that the search for a Christian understanding of man has gone on and must continually go on among apologists in the context of their time and their cultural situation.

In our own time, I have suggested that the pressure for this search is enormous. Alternate views of man which compete with Christian anthropology have gained strength and circulation in the modern world. Scientifically divined accounts of human nature and destiny are resistant to some of the basic presuppositions of traditional Christian anthropology. They demand a holistic view of man that regards as spurious any appeal to a "spiritual" dimension or a relationship to the divine as constituting an intrinsic element of the human makeup. Moreover, the modern understanding of reality in general is temporal and processive. This sort of world view stands as a fundamental challenge to traditional notions about man which were forged in the context of a static world view and an acceptance

of the contrast between history and eternity. Finally, in the midst
of the competition between new and old ideas about man, modern
advances in medicine, science, and technology have created moral
dilemmas concerning the nature and quality of human existence
which have, in turn, prompted many in science and religion alike
to insist upon the need for a clear understanding of the human good.

The theologian-ethicist must be as clear as possible about the
tradition of the past within which he stands. He needs to understand,
sift, and evaluate the ideas to which he is heir. This has been the
purpose of these last three chapters. We need to know how Christians have understood man in order that we may understand both
the rich resources of our past and the problems involved in appropriating them for our present apologetic situation. I have undertaken this
investigation in terms of the doctrine of the image of God since
so much of Christian anthropology has been focused on this theological construct.

What we have seen in the tradition, first of all, has been a tendency
to divide man's being in some significant way. The structural dualisms, which define the image of God in terms of a split between
natural and supernatural, and the dualisms which dichotomize human
existence in terms of history versus eternity both tend to reflect a
heteronomous outlook on reality. Although in all cases the image
of God is in some way related to the total being of man—there
is no radical Greek or Manichean dualism—man is not in fact valued
holistically and his natural and historical existence is subordinate
to his primordial origins and his eternal destiny. The effect of these
dualities on the Christian approach to ethical considerations of
human fulfillment is to de-emphasize creative involvement in the
structures of nature and history in favor of concentration on personal
spirituality and virtue in preparation for or in anticipation of individual salvation in eternity. Obviously, this overall outlook is problematic for the contemporary mind-set which considers temporality
and process to be the principal paradigms for understanding a holistically conceived universe.

The efforts of nineteenth and twentieth century secularizing
theologies have succeeded in eliminating the dualistic notions of the
tradition. They have set nature and history in the center of their
theological concern and sought to define the human good and the

hope of human fulfillment in terms of the potentials that exist within that context. Consequently, the scope of Christian ethics is unrestricted by any sense of other-worldly priorities. Certainly, this sort of theology of man and his world accords quite well with the autonomous attitude that pervades secular culture. However, the price of accommodation is too dear. Secularizing theologies verge on suppressing almost entirely any sense of the Transcendent upon whom man s dependent, by whom he is judged, and in whom he has his ultimate hope. This leads to a virtual reduction of religion to ethics, a reduc tion that grossly underestimates the human predicament of sin. Tha is, it eliminates the one dichotomy which cannot be eliminated in theology and in reality this side of the kingdom of God, the dichotomy between what man is and what he ought to be.

The tradition from Augustine to Tillich provides us with a theonomous view of man. The ontological monism which both share enables us to see man holistically and his universe holistically. It enables us to speak of God and man's relation to God without thinking of God as wholly other than or apart from experienced reality. Rather, God is its ground. Man's sense of relatedness to the divine can be spoken of not simply on the basis of an appeal to religious authority but also in terms of an ontology in which God and Being are one. In many ways, then, this whole approach is one of the most promising resources we have for twentieth century apologetics. This is, of course, especially so in the form given by Tillich in our own time. However, it is vitally important, as Tillich himself recognized, that the roots of his own work are deeply embedded in a catholic tradition that can be traced back to Augustine.

The effects of this theonomous view on the scope of the Christian ethic and its conception of the human good are particularly clear in Tillich's work. When one sees religion as the substance of culture and culture as the form of religion, one is bound to draw at least two conclusions. The first is that there is nothing in the phenomena of culture outside the concern of the Christian ethic. The whole man—personal, historical, natural, and cultural—must be considered in defining the human good. Secondly, the values and imperatives associated with human fulfillment will display a certain cultural relativity even as they reflect an absolute substance. This, of course, is far more amenable to our current sense of relativity in a world of temporal process. However, as we have seen, Augustine dichotomizes man by the disjunction of history and eternity that is apparent in his eschatology and symbolized in his idea of the two cities. In the final analysis Tillich does not overcome this ahistorical bent. Again, it is under the discussion of eschatology that the problem is apparent.

The eschatological question about man appears, then, to be the most stubborn and most pressing one in appropriating the tradition for modern apologetics. We shall deal with this question in Part Two. The entire purpose and justification of this study stands or falls on the answer we receive.

Part Two

The Eschatological
Perspective

Chapter V

The Recovery of Eschatology

In a sense, the title of this chapter is a bit misleading. Eschatology has not been absent from Christian theology at any point in its history. Traditional theologies have always retained a place for a doctrine of "the last things." Modern theologians like Barth and Bultmann have maintained the central importance of eschatology. However, a genuinely historical eschatology which deals with the question of universal history has certainly been neglected and even abandoned. One of the key factors in the recovery of historical eschatology has been the rediscovery of apocalyptic as an authentic and crucial biblical tradition.

ESCHATOLOGY AND APOCALYPTIC: DEVELOPMENTS IN BIBLICAL STUDIES

As Klaus Koch has pointed out in his recent book, it is the heritage of nineteenth century biblical scholarship—particularly as it has affected German Old Testament scholarship—that apocalyptic and apocalyptic eschatology have been carefully distinguished from prophecy and prophetic eschatology. Apocalyptic has been treated as a special case in the development of Israelite and Jewish traditions and one that is decidedly inferior to the tradition of classical prophecy.[1] Similarly, Paul D. Hanson has indicated that, in the past, pre-exilic prophecy has been contrasted with late Jewish apocalyptic due to the method that has been used in comparing the two. Customarily, scholars have compared the characteristics of the two traditions and have concluded from their lack of common elements that apocalyptic must be a late decadent development with no religious worth or a new phenomenon without primary connections to prophetic Yahwism. This supposed discontinuity with primary prophetic traditions has led scholars to seek the origins of apocalyptic in outside influences, chiefly in Persian dualism as mediated by Hellenism.[2] Consequently, apocalyptic has been given short shrift in major Old Testament theologies. Gerhard von Rad's treatment of apocalyptic in the most recent edition of his *Theology of the Old Testament* says little that is positive about its contribution and staunchly retains the distinction of apocalyptic from prophecy. However, his willingness even to discuss it goes beyond the consideration that other German scholars have been willing to give it.[3]

The disdain for apocalyptic in Old Testament studies has, of course, been paralleled in the New Testament field as well. Despite the efforts of Johannes Weiss and Albert Schweitzer to demonstrate that Jesus' central message of the kingdom of God and his own self-understanding were permeated with apocalyptic influences, New Testament scholars continued to teach a nonapocalyptic Jesus. In the Bultmannian tradition apocalyptic is demythologized in favor of the kerygmatic call to decision. Jesus himself is supposed to have been purely kerygmatic in his approach and, therefore, the first demythologizer of the mythical world view of the New Testament, which includes apocalyptic notions. The Bultmannian emphasis, together with reflection on the problem of the delayed parousia, led to realized eschatology as a replacement for the futuristic, historical impulses of apocalyptic. The historical, cosmic eschatology of apocalyptic collapses into the realized eschatology of the personal history of the individual. The retreat from apocalyptic is complete.

In striking contrast to the German assessment, Paul Hanson of Harvard has asserted a definite link between apocalyptic and the prophetic tradition. Hanson claims that apocalyptic is an unbroken inner-Israelite development out of pre-exilic and exilic prophecy. Outside influences come in only as embellishments after Jewish apocalyptic had already developed. Apocalyptic is the mode assumed by prophetic eschatology in the radically altered setting of the post-exilic community. Scholars have failed to see this continuity because they have compared and observed the disparities between the extremes of fully developed apocalyptic literature and the literature of classical prophecy. There were indeed change and development and, therefore, there are decided differences between the two extremes. But they must be understood as extremes on a continuum. The prophet and the apocalyptic visionary both proclaim Yahweh's cosmic sovereignty. The prophet translates this sovereignty in terms of plain history, real politics, and human instrumentality. The apocalyptic visionary in the pessimistic post-exilic situation is not interested in history and politics. However, there is still a fundamental continuity to the basic vision of eschatological hope throughout the history of prophecy and apocalyptic.[4] In sum, Hanson's thesis succeeds in demonstrating the unity of apocalyptic with the entire prophetic tradition while yet providing an understanding of how and why the differences between prophecy and apocalyptic arose due to historical development in Israel.

This sort of positive appraisal of the role of apocalyptic is now becoming more the rule than the exception in current biblical studies. Perhaps no more dramatic a move has been made than that by Ernst Käsemann. His now famous statement, "Apocalyptic was the mother of Christian theology,"[5] shocked the scholarly world that had virtually abandoned apocalyptic. In contrast to his mentor, Rudolf Bultmann, who had reduced the futuristic, eschatological themes of apocalyptic to Heideggerian speculations on the futurity of man, Käsemann contended that this ahistorical reduction of God's future to man's futurity is inappropriate to the pervasive historical orientation of New Testament apocalyptic eschatology. Indeed, apocalyptic's projection of a definite beginning and a definite end to history gave Christianity what it needed to think historically and to create Gospels which present the life of Jesus from an eschatological perspective.[6]

Of course, Carl Braaten is right in observing, as others have, that Käsemann only traces the presence of apocalyptic influence back to Easter and not to the historical Jesus himself. Nonetheless, his evidence of the central importance of apocalyptic in the New Testament is a powerful argument against those who prefer to discount its relevance. Moreover, Professor Braaten believes that if we also consider the work of Ulrich Wilckens we can see how Käsemann's statement that apocalyptic is the mother of Christian theology can be pushed back to encompass the historical Jesus as well. Wilckens does recognize that Jesus was not an apocalyptist. However, he demonstrates that it is only within the framework of the expectations of the apocalyptic tradition that we can grasp the self-understanding of Jesus and the meaning of his life. Jesus certainly cannot be understood as emerging out of the rabbinic tradition when one considers his unprecedented critique of the Torah and his continual adversary relationship with the scribes and Pharisees. Rather, his own perception of his authority to level such a critique at the venerable traditions of rabbinic theology and piety had to have arisen out of an understanding that in his person a new reality had emerged superseding the tradition of the past. Within the framework of apocalyptic, Jesus could understand himself as bringing in a prolepsis of the eschatological kingdom. In view of the fact that the law is a "contingent event of history directed by a personally free God," Jesus, as the eschatological future of God, could claim authority over the law.[7] The notion of Jesus bringing about in his own person a prolepsis of the apocalyptic expectation of the kingdom is crucial to our being able to understand Jesus as linked to apocalyptic. Thus Braaten concludes:

> The fact that many scholars are reluctant to link the eschatology of Jesus with late Jewish apocalyptic may be explained by the fact that Jesus brought about a massive concentration of apocalyptic expectation in his own activity. The apocalyptic outlook on the future is intentionally curved back on the present activity of Jesus. He does not merely point to the future in the present; instead, he makes present the realities of the future in a concentrated way. The attitude that a person takes to Jesus now determines his own personal destiny. This is the material point of continuity between the historical Jesus and the post-Easter kerygma.[8]

In sum, current biblical studies on the role of apocalyptic have now enabled scholars to view apocalyptic, not as a strange aberration outside the mainstream of the biblical tradition, but as a link in the chain of the development of biblical eschatology that begins in the Old Testament and culminates in Jesus and the early Christian church.

SYSTEMATIC DEVELOPMENT:
WOLFHART PANNENBERG

It is the recent renaissance of apocalyptic studies and particularly his contact with Ulrich Wilckens that gave Wolfhart Pannenberg an important impetus for embarking on a theological program which has restored history and eschatology to a prominent place in theology.

In Pannenberg's view it is theology's task "to understand all being in relation to God, so that without God they simply could not be understood. That is what constitutes theology's universality."[9] The universality of the idea of God demands this. However, when theology began to retreat from this vision by restricting its task to a "special-positivism" of Protestantism, it set itself up as one science among others. Consequently, when "secular" sciences make assertions about reality and history that stand at odds with theological tradition, the credibility of theology is open to question. In the face of such questioning, we realize that the dissolution of the traditional doctrine of Scripture at the hands of historical criticism and new hermeneutics has brought on a crisis for theology. Without the doctrine of Scripture as the unassailable source of all truth concerning the realities it deals with, theology is left with an inability to perform its universal task.[10]

However, developments in hermeneutics and the secularization of culture are not the only deterrents to theology's universality. Another source of the problem is certain dualistic tendencies in theology that are akin to the dualisms we have encountered in the preceding discussion of the image of God. Specifically, Pannenberg refers to the effects of the "positivism of revelation" which underlay the rise of Protestant scholasticism. Its origins are to be seen in setting the limits between "a realm of supernatural knowledge and a contrasting realm of so-called natural knowledge."[11] This decision really occurs in the thirteenth century's determination to set Aristotelian philosophy and the Christian tradition side by side but not in a relationship of mutual completion. Notwithstanding the effects of Aquinas's efforts to relate the two, they were easily broken apart by the distinction maintained between them. This division of universal truth and knowledge into two realms of knowledge and two ways of knowing constitutes the historical root of the loss of theology's universality.[12] As I have already pointed out in Part One, this is the epistemological counterpart to a dichotomized view of the *humanum*. It is therefore significant for my overall concern to observe how Pannenberg attacks this dualism in order to assess the value of his solution for a corresponding solution to the problem of the doctrine of man.

The solution Pannenberg offers shows how important the recovery of apocalyptic is for his theology. The restoration of theology's universality cannot be accomplished by a reversion to authoritarian modes of thought.

> Rather, it must be shown to the secular present that its own hope for the future becomes recognizable in the event that was foundational for primitive Christianity, and whose meaning for that time was that the eschatological future of the world and the whole human race has dawned.[13]

As Pannenberg sees it, the possibility for conveying such a vision is dependent upon a return to the notion of universal history. He believes that the eschatological horizon of universal history is that horizon which is the common future uniting the world of the twentieth century with that of the first. Therefore, the question of the possibility of a renewed understanding of universal history must be raised. Can reality itself, in its fundamental aspects, "be understood as historical, and the history of nature and man understood in their unity as the history of God?" The answer is that universal-historical thinking has its origin in the biblical idea of God and that this concept in modern philosophy of history is an inheritance from Jewish apocalyptic and Christian theology of history. It is hard to imagine how the idea of universal history could proceed without the idea of God. Correspondingly, theology can only understand the events recorded in the Bible as events of God if they are seen as related to the totality of all events; that is, universal history. "Thus, even for primitive Christianity, the meaning of the resurrection of Jesus was based on the conviction, held by those contemporaries who lived in apocalyptic expectations, that with this event the end of all things had arrived."[14] In short, the Bible operates with a view of universal history.

The Old Testament and apocalyptic understanding of history stand in contrast to all ahistorical modes of thought. The Old Testament does not see God as merely the origin of ever-repeating cycles of events which constitute reality. Rather, it offers an eschatological, linear view of history as moving toward the goal of the living, participating God. The structure of history is determined by God's promises and the fulfillment of those promises. Apocalyptic extends this structure to cover the whole course of the world from creation to eschaton. It goes beyond the prophets who generally saw the divine goals in inner-historical terms. Apocalyptic saw the goal and meaning of history as fulfilled in its end. Thus, it extended the historical-eschatological outlook of the Old Testament to the proportions of universal history. Apocalyptic and the New Testament both hold fast to and develop the understanding of reality as history which is unfolded in the Old Testament. Acknowledgment of this universal-historical perspective of the Scriptures entails interpreting them in terms of a theocentric view of history. This means that God is the bearer of history, and the destiny of man as an historical being is bound up in the purpose of God for history. The biblical outlook is thus in conflict with the anthropocentric view of history advanced by nineteenth century historicism and, in our century, by Bultmann's concentration on human historicity as the focus of theology.[15]

The universal-historical vision developed in Old Testament, Jewish apocalyptic, and New Testament is crucial to Pannenberg's eschatology and to his concern for restoring the universality of theology. It is within this historical framework that Pannenberg can speak of his well-known idea of the Christ event as the prolepsis of the kingdom of God, the future of history. From this point of view the eschaton is seen as the fulfillment of history, a fulfillment revealed in the Christ. We therefore have a vision of the end, the whole, a perspective from which to view the meaning of events. God is integrally related to history as its future and, therefore, the history of man and nature may be understood in their unity as the history of God.

Pannenberg's ideas can be further amplified by a brief look at some of the salient arguments in his Christology in *Jesus-God and Man*. Pannenberg asserts that Jesus spoke within the context of apocalyptic, eschatological expectations. His proclamation and his claim cannot be extracted from that context. Jesus' claim is basically that a man's *future* salvation is bound up with his decision about Jesus in the *present*. This claim conveys a tension between the futurity of the end of the world and the immediate presence of the final decision about the end in the person of Jesus. The question arises concerning the verification of that claim, and the nature of the claim itself suggests that its verification is expected only from the future. This is the proleptic structure of Jesus' claim.[16] As such, Jesus' claim concerning his own significance for mankind stands firmly within the tradition of prophetic and apocalyptic claims concerning future history. These claims too were subject to verification on the basis of the course of events, as a confirmation aimed at the future verification of his claim to authority.[17]

The resurrection of Jesus is that event of the future which verified the claim of Jesus, demonstrated his unity with God, and, therefore, revealed his divinity as the Son of God. In the context of apocalyptic eschatological expectations and in that context alone could Jesus' resurrection be seen to have made immediate sense to those who witnessed it. The connection between Jesus' resurrection and the apocalyptic eschatological expectation of a universal resurrection of the dead would have been immediately apparent. Moreover, the significance of Jesus' resurrection as an eschatological event for the verification of his pre-Easter claim would also have been evident. Therefore, Pannenberg believes that the resurrection of Jesus would have yielded a number of conclusions for the New Testament Jew, among them that the end of the world had begun, that God had confirmed the pre-Easter activity of Jesus, and that God is ultimately revealed in Jesus.[18] Thus, the resurrection, understood historically within the context of apocalyptic expectations, is the key to Pannenberg's Christology and to his entire eschatological theology. It is the event in which we see Jesus as the prolepsis of the kingdom of God, the revelation of the universal future of history, the revelation of God himself.

As the linchpin of Pannenberg's eschatological theology, the resurrection is also the foundation of his notion of the priority of the future. In the following we have an initial statement of the idea of the priority of the future, which also indicates how Jesus' message, though within the framework of apocalyptic, is still distinctive.

> Our starting point then is the Kingdom of God understood as the eschatological future brought about by God himself. Only in the light of this future can we understand man and his history. God's rule is not simply in the future, leaving men to do nothing but wait quietly for its arrival. No, it is a mark of Jesus' proclamation of the Kingdom of God that future and present are inextricably interwoven. . . . The accent of Jesus' message differed from the Jewish eschatological hope at precisely this point: Jesus underscored the *present impact* of the imminent future.[19]

As I noted in Chapter Three, Bultmann has stressed the present impact of the kingdom but neglected its futurity in the interest of a thoroughly realized eschatology. By contrast, the traditional view-point, while allowing for an already accomplished but not yet con-summated salvation, has stressed the essential futurity of the king-dom of God. That is, while we can say that God's reign is present in the hearts of believers (kingdom of Grace) and that he orders and sustains the universe (kingdom of Power), our understanding of the kingdom as his universal reign (kingdom of Glory) is set over against historical existence as its successor. This is clear, for example, in the paradoxical tension of the two kingdoms doctrine in the Lutheran tradition. Both realized and futuristic eschatology are, as I have tried to demonstrate in Part One, ahistorical. The former is because it reduces eschatology to individual historicity and the latter is because it sets the future over against history.

With the assertion that there is a prolepsis of the kingdom of God (an appearance of the horizon of universal history) in the victory of Jesus, Pannenberg offers a startlingly different eschatology. The proleptic significance of the resurrection is paradigmatic for our over-all understanding of the structure of history and reality and of God's relationship to it. In this conception the future is prior to the present and the past. Past and present have their source in the future, the future being conceived as the continually coming and creative impact of God's future. The structure of reality is proleptic. This, of course, reverses our customary understanding of the future as the product of potentials in the past and present. With this conceptual scheme, Pannenberg has radically eschatologized our understanding of his-tory and radically historicized our understanding of eschatology. The meaning of history is finally in its end but that end, that future of God's kingdom, is prior to every present, revealed definitively in the Christ event, and an ever present creative force drawing history to itself. This is a temporal view of reality and God's relationship to it. A return-to-origins eschatology which grounds the future in a primal past and promises a restoration of the past as the successor to history is precluded by this view. Also precluded is any sort of realized eschatology which relates purely to the individual and offers no promise for the future of history.

Naturally, these brief remarks on Pannenberg's thought beg to be elaborated. It is especially important for this discussion that we see the manner in which Pannenberg's understanding of the proleptic structure of reality correlates with human experience in general. In the face of the contemporary world view, it is already evident that Pannenberg's scheme represents a real gain in its presentation of a temporal understanding of God and the world, which mitigates the dualities that have arisen in the tradition. This is a point I shall develop further as the work progresses. However, is there more that can be said concerning the correlation between proleptic eschatology and man's experience of himself and his world?

As we have seen, it was the apocalyptic, eschatological expectation of the resurrection of the dead that provided the context of meaning for the first Christians to understand the significance of Jesus' resurrection as a prolepsis of the kingdom of God. This hope, borne by the religious traditions of Jesus' time and rooted in the Old Testament, was the point of contact for the message of Jesus' history with man's experience of reality at that time. The question thus arises—especially in light of the strangeness of apocalyptic visions to the eyes of modern man—as to whether or not there is a conceptual structure in modern man's perception of reality and his own existence which includes the same kind of expectations as a point of contact for the proclamation of the resurrection gospel today. Does that which came to expression in apocalyptic hope represent something intrinsic to humankind that continues to find expression in the phenomenon of man?

Pannenberg makes a beginning in his answer to this question by asserting that it is "a generally demonstrable anthropological finding that the definition of the essence of man does not come to ultimate fulfillment in the finitude of earthly life."[20] There is an abiding expectation of life beyond death which can be relinquished only at the expense of our understanding of human life as uniquely individual. Only if man were to think of his life as fulfilled when it has become absorbed in community and the community, in turn, has achieved fulfillment in some way, could man give up hope in life beyond death. However, despite man's creation for community, his individuality is an indelible trait. Consequently, all models of hope for human fulfillment fail to satisfy the human spirit if the hope they project cannot reach beyond the harsh realities of death. This insight is buttressed by modern anthropology when it speaks of man's "openness to the world" or his "environmental freedom." These

concepts indicate the impulse to seek beyond every finite circumstance for the ultimate fulfillment of those drives that constitute his nature. In the unique situation of man knowing of his own
death, this impulse presses the search for the fulfillment of his destiny
beyond the horizon of death.[21]

Beyond this fundamental hope of life after death, the symbolic
concepts which express it ought also express a mode of existence
that is a corollary of the human existence out of which this hope
emerges. The Platonic expression of that hope in the "immortality of
the soul" is no longer tenable in view of man's understanding of himself as a *whole* being. By contrast, hope in the resurrection does, of
course, correspond to our view of man as a psychophysical unity.
Moreover, the hope of the resurrection is also a hope for the
resurrection of the community of mankind, as well as for the individual. In this we find an appreciation for the fact that, although
individuality cannot be absorbed in community, it is also fundamental to humanity that it cannot be fulfilled apart from community. In sum, the phenomenon of human hope offers a point of contact
for the disclosure of the ultimate, eschatological significance of the
resurrection and its implicit promise. At the same time, the resurrection promise offers a hope for man's fulfillment which correlates with the structure of human being out of which human hope
arises. In the traits of human existence and hope we have a point of
continuity with that which came to expression in apocalyptic expectation. It is a point of continuity that overleaps the centuries that
stand between that era and our own.[22]

Ultimately, it is this structure of human hope, as the abiding context for the meaningfulness of the resurrection gospel, that resolves
as well the perennial problem of the delay of the parousia. The
impact of the resurrection victory upon the lives of men is not bound
to the length of intervening centuries between its occurrence and
the promised end of the world. Its validity for us is grounded rather
in this anthropologically interpreted apocalyptic expectation and its
ability to stand the test of time.[23]

SYSTEMATIC DEVELOPMENT:
JÜRGEN MOLTMANN

Toward the beginning of his *Theology of Hope* Jürgen Moltmann
describes the loss of eschatology as a medium of theological thinking

that has resulted from the ascendancy gained by various forms of "transcendental eschatology." Transcendental eschatology takes shape traditionally as the appendix to the dogmatics, the transcendent end that makes no impact upon the present. It takes shape in modern theology in Barth's transcendent eschaton equidistant from all ages, in Bultmann's "eschatological moment," and in Althaus's axiological understanding of the relationship of eternity to time. The transcendental view of eschatology corresponds to Greek thought patterns. The Greeks saw in the *logos* the epiphany of the eternal present of Being as the medium of the universal truth of reality. But in contrast to the *logos* and epiphany of the Greeks stand the promise and *apocalypsis* of the Hebrew and Christian traditions. The restoration of *promise* as the key to unlocking Christian truth will mean the restoration of eschatology as the appropriate medium of theology.[24]

Promise exerts a profound influence on our perception of reality. It constitutes a declaration of the coming of what does not yet exist and, therefore, orients man's life to the future of its expected fulfillment. When it is divine promise, the basis of expectation is not in the potentialities of the present but in the possibilities of what God can do. Hope in divine promise indicates the priority of the future over every past and present, for what is hoped for emanates from God's future rather than the inherent potencies of what already is. As such, promise binds man to the future. "The promise takes man up into its own history in hope and obedience, and in so doing stamps his existence with an historic character of a specific kind."[25] History initiated and determined by promise displays a definite orientation toward the fulfillment of something beyond every past reality. It does not display the pattern of cyclical recurrence. The meaning of the future supersedes and sums up the meaning of the past and present. It stands in contradiction to all reality presently or previously experienced and, consequently, places man into an interval of tension between the revelation of promise and the actuality of fulfillment.[26] In short, with Moltmann as with Pannenberg, eschatology is historicized and history is eschatologized.

This eschatological vision of reality comes to expression when the promise of prophecy reaches the dimensions of a universal eschatology for all mankind that includes the negation of death itself. As such it surpasses all previous horizons of future hope. It becomes truly an eschaton, a *ne plus ultra,* a *novum ultimum.* It is in connection with this zenith point of prophetic promise that Moltmann engages the unfolding theological scheme. Here Moltmann admits to the difficulty of properly understanding the nature of apocalyptic in the light of contradictory opinions among the experts. However, he also admits at the outset that apocalyptic shares with prophecy the same futuristic eschatological outlook. Nonetheless, distinctions must be made between the two traditions. Most important of the differences between apocalyptic and prophetic eschatology is the deterministic or fatalistic dualism displayed by apocalyptic in its setting of one aeon against the other, the world of righteousness, that is coming, against the world under the sway of evil, which is present. Moreover, unlike the prophets the apocalyptist veils his place in history. He does not make his address in terms of the ebb and flow of concrete historical events.[27]

In view of these features of apocalyptic it is understandable that Moltmann should raise the question—one that needs to be raised in any case—as to whether or not apocalyptic represents a non-historic thinking. A positive answer to that question would come from von Rad's assessment of apocalyptic as an expression of earlier cosmological schemata found in myth. A negative answer comes from the "Pannenberg school" which sees it as a first attempt at projecting a vision of universal history that is based upon prophetic eschatology. Both judgments are based upon the cosmological dimensions achieved by apocalyptic. The former sees this indicating that history will come to a standstill. The latter views the cosmological motif as indicating that the category of history should be understood as the medium for seeing an alternative, although its difference from Pannenberg's perspective seems more in the way the statement is devised than in the substance of its consequence for our understanding of apocalyptic. Moltmann allows that apocalyptic may not represent a cosmological interpretation of eschatology but an eschatological historic interpretation of the cosmos:

> It might well be that when the promise becomes eschatological it breaks the bounds even of what aetiology had hitherto considered to be creation and cosmos, with the result that the *eschaton* would not be a repetition of the beginning, nor a return from the condition of estrangement and the world of sin to the state of original purity, but is ultimately wider than the beginning ever was. Then it would not be the case that eschatology becomes cosmological in apocalyptic,

and is thereby stabilized, but *vice versa* cosmology would become eschatological and the cosmos would be taken up in terms of history into the process of the eschaton.[28]

From the viewpoint of apocalyptic,

> The whole world is now involved in God's eschatological process of history, not only the world of men and nations. The conversion of man in the prophetic message then finds its correlate in the conversion of the whole cosmos, of which apocalyptic speaks. The prophetic revolution among the nations expands to become the cosmic revolution of all things.[29]

For Moltmann, then, the answer to the question as to whether or not apocalyptic is nonhistorical in its thought is ultimately a negative one. Rather the eschatological impulses of the prophetic tradition are expanded to cosmic proportions by the eschatologizing of cosmology.

Perhaps most significant of all of our concerns, in light of our previous analysis of the effects of traditional eschatology on the doctrine of the image, is the fact that Moltmann clearly sees apocalyptic representing a breakdown of the return-to-origins eschatology of the mythological mind-set which is so typical of the majority view in the history of Christian thought. This insight is taken up into his own assessment of the Christian tradition as he pursues the case for his theology of hope. Hope, Moltmann believes, has suffered the impediment of being bound for centuries to a Christian understanding of history that reflects the pattern of the myth of the eternal return: "History is 'paradise lost'; salvation, 'paradise regained.' " The lost origin that man remembers in his suffering in this world is restored by church and faith. Grace brings a return to the integrity of the primordial source at the beginning of history. This has characterized the tradition, and "dialectical theology" has not succeeded in breaking its spell. However, notwithstanding these facts, the insight for breaking down this cyclical view resides within the tradition's understanding of grace itself. Irenaeus, Athanasius, and Augustine all realized that, ultimately, grace is the grace of a *new* creation, not simply one in which sin is overcome but one in which the very necessity and possibility of sin are overcome. This is "more" than a renewal of the original. The category of the *novum* in an eschatological theology, such as we have seen unfolding out of Moltmann's reflec-

tions on prophetic promise and apocalyptic, placards this hidden
category of the "re" which has dominated theology and historical
thinking in general through such concepts as renaissance, revolution,
revival, renewal, restoration.[30]

The category of the *novum* is indeed a major concept in Moltmann's whole eschatological outlook. The *novum* expresses the fact
that an eschatologically oriented faith is not interested in the primordial *proton* of reality as an explanation of its nature. It is interested instead in the new future that will change and transform the
world. "This eschatological attitude toward the world creates history
instead of interpreting nature." The *novum* also refers to the fact that
in Paul's view the new creation in Christ is something that takes up
into itself the old creation even as it surpasses it. The future perceived
under the rubric of the *novum* is open and free in correspondence
with the freedom of God. This is implicit also in Paul's understanding of the new as more than mere renewal but the entrance of something unexpected.[31] It is the resurrection that brings this radically
new thing to pass. This is the miracle whose newness, Moltmann is
continually fond of saying, corresponds to a *creatio ex nihilo*. Indeed,
for Moltmann as well as Pannenberg, Christianity stands or falls on
the reality of the resurrection. Consequently, although Moltmann
wants to make the differences clear between the content of apocalyptic
hope and what comes to expression in the Christ,[32] he is nonetheless
clear that it was within the horizon of apocalyptic hope that the
significance of the Easter event came to be recognized and pro-
claimed.[33] Moreover, it is this resurrection of Jesus which anticipates
the universal eschatological horizon projected by apocalyptic.[34] The
category of the *novum* in Moltmann's theology fleshes out even
further and in somewhat different language the understanding of
history that we find developed in Pannenberg under the rubric of the
ontological priority of the future.

In both Pannenberg and Moltmann reality is perceived as historical.
It is oriented toward the universal eschatological future and is indeed
a product of the "new" that breaks in from that future as contingent
or unexpected event generated out of the freedom of God who is the
power of the future. The meaning and fulfillment of reality and, therefore, of human existence are to be sought neither in its primordial
origin nor in a return to those origins. It is sought rather in the

arrival of the "not yet," the kingdom of God, proleptically revealed in the crucified and risen Christ. He provides in his victory over death the content of universal hope and the horizon of universal history. Gone is the static hierarchical model of reality which characterized the thinking of the past and which was bound to lead to dualisms dividing our understanding of man's nature between his earthbound nature and his transcendental, supernatural, suprahistorical destiny. The new paradigm of transcendence is the future.[35] Our understanding of reality has been set on its side to reflect the linear perspective of a temporal view of reality instead of the two-story design which reflects a static, spatial concept of reality. The understanding of existence from the Christian perspective shifts from the static permanence of the cathedral to the becoming change expressed in the metaphor of a ship that is on its way to harbor but not yet there.[36]

CONCLUSION: TOWARD A NEW THEONOMY

The restoration of apocalyptic to an important role in our understanding of biblical eschatology, the recovery of biblical eschatology in general, and the systematic efforts of men like Pannenberg and Moltmann, all serve to provide us with a comprehensive eschatological theology. Within this enlarged theological framework one can now interpret the biblical materials specifically related to the doctrine of man in a reconstruction under the rubric of the image of God that is thoroughly eschatological in its orientation.

In terms of the analysis of Part One, what I am seeking in the reconstruction of Christian anthropology is a new theonomy, a way of understanding man from the Christian perspective that overcomes the heteronomous tendencies of "dichotomized man" and the autonomous tendencies of "secularized man" while yet dealing more adequately with the questions of history and temporal process than the theonomous outlook of the tradition from Augustine to Tillich. I believe that Pannenberg and Moltmann have set us on the way to a new theonomy. When God is conceived as the future of history, and reality is seen as historical and proleptic in structure according to the ontological priority of the future, then God is neither outside reality and history nor is man the bearer of history in a universe which excludes the transcendent. Rather, God, as the "power of the future"

(Pannenberg's term), is the Alpha and Omega of every past and present, the ontological *prius* and the universal fulfillment of historical, becoming reality. As such, God is "the ground of all being" in Tillichian terms, except that our understanding of him as the "ground" is reshaped in terms of history and temporal process under the impulse of biblical eschatology.

Chapter VI

The Image of God
and Eschatology

The variety of teaching concerning the *imago Dei* which we have sampled from the history of Christian thought becomes understandable when one studies the scriptural evidence on which it is based. The direct references in Scripture to the image of God are relatively few compared with other important biblical concepts. Moreover, the relevant texts of both Old and New Testaments are not so straightforward and consistent in meaning as would be required for an unambiguous interpretation of the cumulative evidence. An interpretive struggle is necessary to insure a viable presentation of what the Bible means by the image of God. Therefore, it is not surprising that the tradition should reflect a wide divergency of positions rather than a unity. However, this situation notwithstanding, the efforts of biblical scholars in recent years, though not providing an unassailable consensus on the nature of the image of God, have at least set certain boundaries within which the interpretation of the image must proceed. The purpose of this chapter is to present in a brief and summary fashion some of the noteworthy results of this scholarship. The results, I believe, will demonstrate that much of the dualism we have observed in the tradition is not biblical and that there is an eschatological orientation to the biblical concept of man that has not yet been fully appreciated.

MAN AS A PSYCHOPHYSICAL UNITY

I think it is fair to say that the tradition of Christian thought has never really lost the idea that the Bible sees man as a unity and that his whole being is the good creation of God. However, I do think, as I have tried to show earlier, that dualistic interpretations of the *imago Dei* have obscured that unity and have, therefore, left us with a problem in presenting a Christian apologetic for the human good in a contemporary world committed to seeing man holistically. It is therefore helpful to remind ourselves that modern biblical scholarship has reemphasized the fact that the image doctrine refers to the whole person as a psychophysical unity.

The Hebrew for "image" is the word *tselem*, which occurs seventeen times in the Old Testament, five of these instances in references to man as the image of God (Gen. 1:26, 27; 5:3; 9:6). In the occurrences of *tselem* which do not deal with man, ten clearly have the meaning of a carved or hewn statue, a copy or facsimile such as an idol. This is the meaning of the root in both the Hebrew and the Aramaic. In the remaining two cases (Pss. 39:6(7); 73:20) the meaning appears to be that of "shadow" or "dream." The consensus of scholarship is that the meaning of *tselem* in Genesis passages dealing with man should retain, in the first instance, its concrete, root meaning of a carved or hewn figure, a copy, while yet allowing for the need to be flexible in the interpretation of the intended meaning of the context.[1]

In Gen. 1:26 the word *demut* (likeness) appears as a modifier and interpreter of *tselem,* indicating the idea of correspondence or similarity. *Demut* can also denote "copy" but it is weaker and more abstract, tempering, perhaps, the idea from mythological backgrounds that *tselem* indicates a purely physical copy such as an idol.[2] However, von Rad notes that the concrete, physical nature of the image, which is the original force of *tselem*, is still very much present in the Priestly writer's theological reflection. There is no reason, therefore, to overspiritualize or intellectualize the concept of the image. Simply to locate the image of God in man's "personality," "dignity," "ability for moral decision," or the like is to think of man in terms of an anthropology that is alien to the Old Testament. The Old Testament thinks of man as a psychophysical whole. Therefore, the marvel of man's physical being is not to be excluded from the image concept. Indeed, Israel may well have conceived of Yahweh as having human form.[3]

However, Israel did not think of God in anthropomorphic terms; they thought of man as theomorphic. This underscores the fact that in the creation narrative man is created in a special relationship of immediacy to God. Von Rad emphasizes that in the P account of creation the portrayal of it as creation-by-word gives the distinct impression of a sharp separation between God and his creation which, at the same time, serves to highlight the special place given to man. The various parts of the created world stand at different points of remove with respect to the immediacy of their relationship to God. The plants, for example, have an indirect relationship to God mediated through the ground which was commissioned to participate in their creation. The animals also have their immediate relationship to the soil. However, nothing stands between God and man. Man was created not by word in the same fashion as the rest but by special resolve in the heart of God. Indeed, the world was created for him.[4]

At the same time, it should be emphasized that there is an infinite difference between God and man in the Hebrew mind.[5] Neither the notion of man's theomorphic creation nor that of his special place in creation nor that of his relationship of immediacy to God should be construed to suggest that the Old Testament offers a doctrine of the dignity and worth of man by using the image concept to highlight noble qualities possessed by man. The action in the creation account is from God to man. God is the prototype and the original; man is but the image and likeness of that original. The studious avoidance of anthropomorphisms in the P account, the emphasis on God's creative initiative, and the concrete thrust of *tselem*, which suggests man's derivative, theomorphic character, all combine to suggest that "that which is peculiarly man's, the real and true manhood of man is a mystery which comes from God."[6] The intent of the image notion seems clearly to indicate that the pattern and fulfillment of man's being, his true identity as man, is to be sought outside the created order. In consequence of his immediacy to God and dependency on God, it follows that man cannot seek the fulfillment of his humanity either in nature or in himself.

As we shall see a little later in this discussion, the insight that man created in the image of God is man as a psychophysical unity is reinforced in the New Testament. Our hope for fulfillment in the image is a hope that awaits its ultimate realization in the resurrection, which, of course, is a resurrection of the whole person. Moreover, inasmuch as this hope is dependent upon a unity with God in Christ mediated through the grace of baptism, the notion of human fulfillment as a function of man's immediate relationship to God is also carried forward in the New Testament. The grace on which this hope depends further underscores the divine initiative and human dependency.

IMMEDIACY, PERSONHOOD, DEPENDENCY

That man is commissioned by God to have dominion over the rest of creation is an idea we meet in both the Priestly and Jahwist accounts of creation. Because it is closely associated with the *imago Dei,* it is a helpful point of inquiry for our further understanding of the biblical view of man. For von Rad and most other commentators, man's dominion over the rest of creation is a function of the purpose of the divine likeness and not its substance. Man is called upon to *represent* God's sovereignty in the nonhuman world. Indeed, the concrete character of *tselem,* which in the first instance serves to alert us that man's physical constitution is included in the image, in this instance helps convey the representative nature of man's dominion:

> The close relation of the term for God's image with that for the commission to exercise dominion emerges quite clearly when we have understood *tselem* as a plastic image. Just as powerful earthly kings, to indicate their claim to dominion, erect an image of themselves in the provinces of their empire where they do not personally appear, so man is placed upon earth in God's image as God's sovereign emblem. He is really only God's representative, summoned to maintain and enforce God's claim to dominion over the earth.[7]

By serving to emphasize the representational nature of human dominion, this analogy is helpful in underscoring the *dependent* and derivative character of man's being which, as we have seen, is also implicit in the idea of an "image." However, beyond that, the fact that man's creation in the image of God fits him for this representational role suggests something more about the substance of the image, something that we can discern if we shift the focus to man's special place of immediacy to God.

The immediacy of the relationship between God and man is certainly no more intensely expressed than in the idea of covenant which is sustained throughout the Bible. Both Israel and the New Israel experience God as a personal Thou, and in Genesis 1 the

Priestly writer succeeds in bringing to life this personhood of God. What is revealed here is God's determination by special resolve to be in fellowship with his noblest creature. He is distinguished from the rest of creation by his being made for an I-Thou relationship with God.[8] He is God's *vis-à-vis*.[9] It follows, then, that for man to be created in the divine likeness means that on him is bestowed the characteristic of personhood or personality.[10] This constitutes his essential "humanness" and is, as such, not a quality or capacity bestowed on man in addition to his humanity. Indeed, all man's distinctive capacities such as reason, freedom, and moral sensibility are to be seen not as ontic qualities comprising some notion of a "natural" as opposed to "supernatural" image of God. Rather, such distinctive qualities are dimensions of human personhood which, in turn, finds its meaning in being the ground of that special, immediate relationship with God which is God's gift to man in creation. "He [man] has a share in the personhood of God; and, as being capable of self-awareness and of self-determination, he is open to the divine address and capable of responsible conduct."[11] It is this capacity for responsible conduct that enables us to understand dominion as a function of the *imago Dei*. It also alerts us to the fact that there is in this commission to sovereignty an implicit imperative to love and rule the earth responsibly as a true reflection of God's care for his creation.[12] The Bible's understanding of man's response to this implicit command to responsible stewardship of the creation leads us to a further amplification of the characteristics of the image concept that we have already seen develop.

THE IMAGE OF GOD AND SIN

Edmund Jacob sees the derivative and representative nature of man's dominion as an appropriate juncture to comment on the manner in which the image concept helps us understand the nature of sin:

> . . . the *imago Dei* means for man a relationship with and dependence upon the one for whom he is only the representative. To wish to be like God, the temptation suggested by the serpent, is to desire to abandon the role of image and on several occasions the Old Testament shows that in behaving thus man degrades himself and falls to the animal level. . . . To remain an image man must maintain his relationship with God, he must remember that he is only

an ambassador and his dominion over creation will be effective only
in proportion as that relationship becomes more real.[13]

As we have observed throughout this discussion, man's existence
is totally dependent upon God. The concept of the image of God
conveys this in seeing man as constituted by his intimate and
immediate relationship with God expressed in terms of a derivative
likeness to God. Sin, as rebellion against God, constitutes a rejection
of that relationship and a refusal to remain in a representational
role. Thus, concerning the Fall, von Rad observes: "Man has stepped
outside the state of dependence; he has refused obedience and
willed to make himself independent. The guiding principle of his life
is no longer obedience but his autonomous knowing and willing,
and thus he has really ceased to understand himself as creature."[14]

What then can we say about the effects of sin upon the image?
To what conclusions are we led when we look at the nature of the
image and the nature of sin side by side? Scholars are virtually
unanimous in their conclusion that the Old Testament does not speak
of a loss of the image of God. In Gen. 5:3 the Priestly writer indicates
that Adam passes the image of God in which he was created to his
son Seth and throughout his generations. Further, in Genesis 9, where
the context is the covenant made with Noah after the flood, the
language of Genesis 1 is clearly echoed and the statement is made
in verse 6, "Whoever sheds the blood of man, by man shall his blood
be shed; for God made man in his own image." Those passages which
are undeniably linked together in the Priestly writer indicate that the
image of God in man remains despite the Fall. In similar fashion, 1
Cor. 11:7 and Jas. 3:9 refer to man as the image of God with no hint
that the image has been lost.[15]

At the same time, it hardly needs documenting that the Bible is
eloquent in its expression of man's sinfulness and the corruption of
his heart. It even equates the fate of man with that of the beasts in
several striking passages (Ps. 49:13, 21; Eccles. 3:19). Indeed, the
account of the Fall itself seems to suggest that it may well be interpreted as a revolt against the *imago Dei* on man's part. Even
though the Jahwist does not use the term *tselem* of God, there are two
factors which enable us to conclude that this is essentially what is at
stake. The first consideration stems from what we have already
observed about the image in the Priestly writer: it refers to man as a

psychophysical whole. The Jahwist portrays the creation of man by using the imagery of God, like a potter, shaping man from the dust of the earth. Man becomes a living *nephesh* (soul, person) when the breath of Yahweh is breathed into his nostrils. As Edvin Larsson has demonstrated, the creative act of uniting the breath of Yahweh, "the breath of life" (*nishmath chayim*), with the dust of the earth to produce a living *nephesh* indicates rather strongly that *nephesh* denotes the same psychophysical unity conveyed by the terms *tselem* and *demut*.[16] This conclusion enables us to connect the two creation traditions and to presume, then, that the image *concept* is involved in the Fall account as well. The second factor is the account of the Fall itself. Gen. 3:5 is crucial here: "For God knows that when you eat of it your eyes will be opened, and you will be like God, knowing good and evil." To desire to be like God is to revolt against the role of being the image of God.

There may well be an echo of this interpretation of the Fall in what appears to be the implicit Adam-Christ typology of Phil. 2:6–11. In this text we learn that Christ, who was in the "form" (*morphe*) of God, willingly took the "form" of a servant, the likeness of man, in order to be our sacrifice. In the New Testament the term for image is *eikon*. As I shall point out later in this chapter, when this term is referred to Christ, it is a divine predicate. The parallelism of verses 6a and 6b shows us that *morphe Theou* is here defined as "equality with God." Thus, it appears that here in Philippians 2 *morphe* has the same force as *eikon* does when the latter is a predicate of Christ. The equivalency of *eikon* and *morphe* is strengthened by the further observation that the Septuagint translates the root *tselem* both as *morphe* (Dan. 3:19) and *eikon* (Gen. 1:26–27). Given this equivalency and the implication it bears that Philippians 2 contains an implicit Adam-Christ contrast, the message of the text might well be paraphrased to read something like this: "Christ who was the very form of God (*morphe* = *eikon* = divinity), unlike Adam who was only the image and likeness of God, did not insist on the prerogatives of his divinity but chose to become less for our sakes, whereas Adam sought to be more than he was for his own sake."

It would seem, then, that we are faced with the possibility of a contradiction in the biblical view of man. On the one hand, we have no indication of a loss of the image being spoken of. On the other hand, we have ample indication of man's rejection of what the image stands for. As a commentary on Gen. 1:26–27, Psalm 8 can be of some help to us at this juncture. The psalm speaks of man as being made a little lower than the angels and being given dominion over the creation. This is further evidence that the image remains despite sin. Yet, it must be realized that the emphasis of the psalm is praise to the majesty of God. Thus, verse 4 raises the question, "What is man that thou art mindful of him . . . ?" The implication of the question is that whatever honor and power man does have are solely the gift of God. Man's dignity resides in his being given the privilege and blessing of wielding power and authority derived from his Creator. Man is image of God but he is *only* image of God! Psalm 8 reinforces the derivative and dependent nature of man's being in the divine likeness. Man can remain in the image of God despite sin because the image is not a possession of man or in his province to dispense with. It is a decision that God makes in his creation, and God remains true and faithful to his intention in creation throughout the history of his dealings with his creatures.[17]

Helmut Thielicke puts the matter in a helpful perspective when he explains that, even though the form of its existence constitutes a theological problem in view of man's rebellion, the image is not something that can be done away with, for it is something God has undertaken to project and create. Man retains it despite sin but he does so in a "negative mode." Therefore,

> The *imago Dei* is a *character indelibilis,* in both the positive and negative mode. . . . But this negative mode of the *imago,* being merely a mode, still bears witness to the existence of the *imago,* and is therefore different in principle for the image's nonexistence or ceasing to be. . . . This indelible character, maintained even in the negative mode of the *imago Dei,* may finally be stated as follows. Man cannot get rid of his humanity. He cannot dehumanize himself. If he could this would imply his ability actually to reach the bestial sphere beyond good and evil which he seeks to attain. But this is exactly what he cannot do.[18]

Thielicke's conclusion is consistent with the personal-relational character of the image of God that we have seen clearly emerging here. When the image has been identified with something other than this, it has led to the structural dualisms we have previously observed. If the image is defined as a supernatural endowment of grace (*donum gratia superadditum*) which perfects nature and enables supernatural good, then sin and Fall spell the loss of this image. However, to the extent that the distinctive qualities of human personhood remain despite sin and are understood as related to the image concept, one is required to posit, as Aquinas did, a natural image that abides in man after the Fall, thereby establishing in man the duality of natural and supernatural. If, with the Reformers, one interprets the image as original righteousness, then the Fall signals its loss. This is, as we saw in the case of Luther, a corollary of the central doctrine of justification, *sola gratia* and *sola fide*. However, again, to the extent that the distinctive qualities of personhood remain and are understood as related to the image concept, one is required to posit, as the Reformers did, some relic of the image that remains despite the Fall, thereby giving us an echo of the Scholastic twofold image.

It is certainly the case that "righteousness" in the sense of a right relationship of communion and union with God is an obvious concomitant of the personal-relational character of the image of God. It is also clear that the Fall and sin are a rebellion against and an alienation from genuine communion and union with God. However, these observations do not obviate our recognition of the fact that man is and remains a being whose nature and destiny are constituted by being created as a person-in-immediate-relationship-with-God. This is the force of Thielicke's point. In its positive mode the image is authentically fulfilled in the establishment of right relationship with God in Christ by grace through faith. In its negative mode it is the rebellion of man's sin against that relationship. This is the essence of man's fallenness and loss of righteousness. It is not, however, a loss of the image but a shift in its mode of being. However, inasmuch as the Reformers, particularly Luther, thought of the original righteousness of the image in thoroughly personalistic, relational terms, their impulses were basically correct. Even their teaching that the Fall meant the loss of the image of God was right-minded as a protest against the Scholastic twofold image which left man with certain natural capacities by which he might cooperate in his salvation.[19]

Thielicke's view is not a rejection of the Reformation outlook, but a reformulation of it which carries forward its essential theological

insights while yet offering an interpretation of the image that more
precisely accords with the biblical witness. In so doing it helps to
mitigate the structural dualities of both the Scholastic and Reformation traditions. Indeed, the idea of the image of God as a perfection
of the primal state lost in the Fall and ultimately restored in eternity
also fosters the sort of ahistorical return-to-origins eschatology that
depreciates the value of historical human existence in the intervening
period between Fall and eschatological restoration. This effect is per·
haps no more vividly illustrated than in Irenaeus's idea of salvation
as the recapitulation of the lost similitude which I discussed earlier.
And, as I also observed at the end of Chapter Four, the dualism
between history and suprahistory which stems from ahistorical
eschatology is the most tenacious of all the dualities involved in the
doctrine of man.

However, interestingly enough, the recapitulation motif of Irenaeus
does not represent the full extent of his thinking on man, history, and
eschatology. As I have already mentioned in passing, Gustav Wingren
has made a persuasive case for the fact that Irenaeus also held to a
futuristic eschatology in which the Christ event enables the *fulfillment*
and *perfection* of the creation which was imperfect or incomplete
at its origin. To begin with, Wingren maintains that, regardless of the
way in which he has been interpreted, Irenaeus did not teach that the
pattern of restoration implicit in his theology of recapitulation was a
restoration of a lost, primal *donum superadditum* or a lost original
righteousness. Rather, Irenaeus saw the restoration in Christ as the
freeing of man from that which perverts his humanity in order that
he may again be truly human. This interpretation in itself goes a long
way toward breaking down the idea of an ahistorical return-to-origins
approach to soteriology and eschatology. More importantly, Wingren
observes that, for Irenaeus, what appears in the incarnation of Christ
is essentially the fulfillment or perfection of the creation which was
imperfect or incomplete at its beginning. Accordingly, Christ is *the*
image of God and, following Col. 3:10, men who are created
in the image and likeness of God ultimately become so in unity with
Christ. To the extent that Irenaeus does teach a restoration motif,
it would appear, then, that we have an apparent contradiction in his
thought: the pattern of "loss and recovery" stands in contrast to that
of "imperfect beginning to perfection." Wingren believes that the

contradiction is resolved in the concomitant concepts of "child" and "growth." For Irenaeus, man at the beginning of creation is like a child. Like a child he is both the same and yet different from what he will be when he is grown. Created as a child, man is not yet completed as God's creation:

> It is the distinctive characteristic of a child that he grows and becomes. This is exactly the same idea as the one which we saw above: man is created in the *imago* and *similitudo* of God, but he is not God's *imago* and *similitudo*—only the eternal Son is that, and only he possesses the whole of God's fullness in Himself. Man is created for the Son, and he attains his perfection in the Son. His destiny was realized only when the image of God took human life in the Incarnation and took up into himself the man who had been created in the image of God. The Incarnation and its benefits had no reality when man was first created: man, therefore, is a child, son, whose goal and objective is full growth.[20]

This statement indicates that for Irenaeus there was no doctrine of man's state of original perfection or righteousness. Wingren points out that a theology of man's original perfection does not emerge until the Augustinian-Pelagian controversy. Prior to that one finds hardly any discussion of the perfections of primordial, paradise man. In this Irenaeus is joined by modern scholars like Walther Eichrodt who maintains that the Old Testament admits of no doctrine of original righteousness in terms of a description of man's primal state.[21] Similarly, J. N. Thomas has observed that the notion of an original righteousness lost in the Fall would not have emerged out of the biblical texts themselves. Rather, it must be accounted for as an inference from the strict Augustinian doctrine of original sin.[22]

Thus, for Irenaeus, the child-likeness of man at the beginning of creation is a matter of innocence and willing dependence rather than the fullness of righteousness and perfection. Man at creation is still man on the way to the goal of his destiny. His growth in Christ toward this goal is indeed God's act of creation. The grace of God's work in creation and salvation is thus merged in the idea of *growth*. At the same time, since a child is in a certain sense the same person he will be at the fullness of his growth and since a child can undergo changes that retard or threaten his growth (in our context, the fall into sin), the correction of these retarding and destructive changes can be understood as a restoration of his original state of being. This would

then account for the fact that the redemption in Christ can also appear
to portray a cyclical pattern of loss and recovery. In this fashion
Wingren demonstrates how Irenaeus's two seemingly contradictory
patterns of salvation and eschatology can be held together as a unified
thought process in the concepts of "child" and "growth."[23] Therefore, it is possible to conclude that Irenaeus understood the image of
God in futuristic eschatological terms. This leads us into the final
segment of the present chapter.

THE IMAGE OF GOD AND
ESCHATOLOGICAL HOPE

We have just observed how man the sinner is continually at odds
with his own being as the image of God. In his book *Man in the Old
Testament*, Eichrodt, among other things, details God's struggle to
overcome this rebellion and establish the personal I-Thou relationship intended by man's creation in the image. Thus, he sees the
theology of the Exodus and of the prophets as complementing the
theology of creation. The Creator and Lawgiver is always, at the
same time, the Redeemer and the God of promise.[24] The individual,
created for communion with God, in direct analogy with the chosen
people, is continually confronted with his failure to respond to that
destiny and, thus, is continually thrown back upon his need for the
redemptive action of God. Eichrodt believes that it is the experience
of divine promise as an answer to this need for a virtual new creation
of God that is projected in the paradise story of creation.[25] Consequently, it is not fanciful to say that, for the Old Testament, the
vision of man created in the image of God is a vision of promise
equal to, if not more than, a vision of origin.

A conclusion of this sort can be given further credence when one
considers von Rad's thesis that Israel's creation theology was worked
out and understood in the context of an already established salvation theology.[26] Discounting the Jahwist account, which does not
treat the creation of the world, we are left with Deutero-Isaiah, the
Priestly document, and several psalms as the Old Testament sources
concerning creation. All of these are late documents. Since it seems
impossible to believe that Israel never thought of Yahweh as Creator
until after the sixth century, one may surmise that the lateness of its

creation theology was due to the time it took Israel to connect creation with the tradition which was peculiarly Israel's, salvation history. Unlike the Canaanites, Israel did not conceive of divine blessing and sustenance as proceeding from the natural environment mythically understood. For Israel, God revealed himself in history. Because of special historical experiences, Yahwism in ancient Israel regarded itself exclusively as a religion of salvation. Von Rad's comments on Deutero-Isaiah are instructive in this regard:

> Thus in, for example, Is. XLV. 5 or XLIII. 1 he uses, in subordinate clauses, hymnlike descriptions of Jahweh such as "he who created the heavens," "He who created you, who formed you," but only to pass over in the principal clause to a soteriological statement, "fear not, I redeem thee." Here, and also in Is. XLV. 25b–28, the allusion to the creator stands in a subordinate clause or in apposition —obviously it has a subordinate function in the prophet's message and does not anywhere appear independently: It is intended to reinforce confidence in the power of Jahweh and his readiness to help. . . . *The reason why the allusion to creation strengthens confidence is that Deutero-Isaiah obviously sees a saving event in the creation itself.*[27]

Von Rad sees the same sort of interweaving of creation and salvation theology in psalms like 89 and 74. And, on the strength of the overall evidence, he thinks it very likely that a soteriological understanding of creation is at the basis of both the P and J accounts of creation. In neither document do we find creation presented for its own sake. Both represent creation as incorporated in a course of history that leads to the call of Abraham and ends with the entry of Israel into Palestine. In this way the beginning of salvation history is put back to creation and creation is regarded as a saving work of Yahweh. This means that creation is a work of Yahweh in history, a work within time, and, as such, "it has ceased to be myth, a timeless revelation taking place in a natural cycle."[28]

If we apply these insights specifically to the creation of man in the image of God, we are able to understand the personal communion and union with God that constitute the image as a hope bound up with the eschatological expectation of Yahweh's deliverance and are characteristic of Old Testament soteriology in general. In view of this, an interpretation of biblical salvation history based on a circular pattern of return-to-origins—paradise, Fall (image of God lost), fallen history, restoration of paradise lost (restoration of lost image) through Christ—would not provide as accurate a context for understanding the biblical view of man as would a future fulfillment motif.

When we turn to the New Testament treatment of the image of God, we find its orientation to be even more clearly eschatological. Beyond the two verses cited earlier (1 Cor. 11:7; Jas. 3:9), which echo the Old Testament in referring straightforwardly to man as the image of God, the New Testament applies the image concept to the person of Christ and to the Christian hope in Christ for the ultimate fulfillment of our humanity. In both instances, the perspective is decidedly eschatological. We can observe this twin focus in 2 Cor. 3:18–4:6 where *eikon* is used of both the Christian (3:18) and of the Christ (4:4). Here Paul is defending his apostolate and the authority of his proclamation by asserting that in his kerygma God himself is revealed through the preaching of Christ, who is the very "image of God" (*eikon tou Theou*). Here image takes the meaning of Revealer and Savior. Christ is the image of God in the unique sense that in him God is most fully revealed; his presence, his "glory," is made known in his gracious action toward men. Through the power of this revelatory kerygma, men are brought to Christ and transformed in the image of God, becoming actual "copies" of the image of which Christ is the prototype.[29] This transformation is not to "an image of an image." Rather, since "image" used of Christ is a divine predicate, transformation in his likeness is virtually fulfillment in the image of *God* as we understand it in Genesis 1. Thus, in the process of defending the revelatory character of his gospel, the apostle has given us a christological, soteriological interpretation of the creation account. The eschatological element of this interpretation becomes apparent when we see further evidence that it is the *resurrected* and *exalted* Christ that Paul speaks of as image of God and that the ultimate transformation of the believer in the image of God is an eschatological hope for his own resurrection.

Paul's argument in the larger context of 2 Cor. 3:18–4:6 is that the revelatory quality of his proclamation is analogous to the revelatory quality of the Christ he proclaims. The believer who comes to know Christ in his gospel sees and is affected by God himself.[30] Such a revelatory and salutary and divine significance obviously could only be attributed to the designation of Christ as the *eikon tou Theou* from the perspective of his "eschatological" victory and exaltation. Certainly, this is the perspective of Philippians 2 ("God has highly exalted him," v. 9) in which context Paul speaks of Jesus as having emptied himself of his divine prerogatives as one who was in "the *form* of God" (v. 6). This is also the perspective of 2 Cor. 3:18–4:6. It is Christ as exalted, as Lord, as Spirit, who is the *eikon* here (see also Rom. 8:29; 1 Cor. 15:45–46, 49). Consequently, one can say that inasmuch as the New Testament references to Christ as the image of God are clearly divine predicates, they are statements of the meaning of his eschatological victory over death for our understanding of his person. This corresponds to Pannenberg's reasoning, which we reviewed in the previous chapter, that in Jesus' milieu his resurrection would be readily perceived as an eschatological event, a prolepsis of the kingdom of God and, therefore, a vindication of Jesus' pre-Easter claim that in him God is revealed.

Thus, in Col. 1:15–20 the christological affirmation concerning the *eikon tou Theou* is that of Christ as preexistent image of God, as Creator and Cosmocrator (vv. 15–17). We see the same notion expressed in Heb. 1:3, 6–13 and in 2:6ff. where, in addition, we note that Christ's lordship is projected as an eschatological event. This eschatological thrust is present in Paul as well, for (in 1 Cor. 15:24–28) the cosmic extent of Christ's reign is also projected as an eschatological event in the process of coming. In that "in him all things were created" (Col. 1:16) and "in him the fullness of God was pleased to dwell" (1:19), we are able to say that "God in Christ" is the force of *eikon* here.[31]

From both Rom. 8:28–30 and 1 Cor. 15:44–49 it is clear that the focus for the ultimate hope of the fulfillment of humanity, which is the fulfillment of our new creation in the image of God, is the resurrection. In the resurrection will be the completion of what is already inaugurated (2 Cor. 3:18), the conformity of the Christian to the image of God in Christ. In becoming thus fully the image of Christ who, as divine image, is our prototype, the whole person will be fully the image of God, as intended by God from the beginning. In 1 Cor. 15:44–49, in particular, we see that the old man, the man of dust who is the "physical" man, is overcome by the new man, who is the heavenly man in whom will be the resurrection to a "spiritual" body. It is this image that the Christian will bear, the image of the resurrected and exalted Christ. In the resurrection of the Christian to imperishable life we have a reproduction of the Christ event in the life of the believer. As in baptism, where the new creation entails dying and rising again with Christ, so also in the resurrection the old man represented by Adam, the man of death, is supplanted by our unity with the new Adam.[32]

Robin Scroggs is correct when he asserts that Christ, the last Adam, assures our eschatological humanity. His resurrection, which is the central motif of Paul's theology, is the pattern for our hope, and the "body of glory" that is therein promised is our true humanity.[33] Friedrich Horst has put the matter this way:

> All the gifts of God promised to the Christian and, therefore, the sum total of all gifts described in his possession of the divine image await their fulfillment in the future Kingdom of God. But all this future is anticipated in Christ, is made present in him.[34]

Here, then, we discern that the full humanity of man, which is only achieved in union with Christ, is essentially future.

The New Testament *eikon* sayings are cloaked in a futuristic eschatology. When we couple this observation with the previous insight that creation theology in the Old Testament can be properly understood within the framework of future promise, we begin to see a consistent pattern of future-orientation in connection with human fulfillment in the image of God. This stands in tension with the old thesis that the Bible presents a circular view of history in which *Endzeit* is a return to *Urzeit*. In this view the eschatological fulfillment of the image would be thought of as a recovery of the primordial past, rather than the realization of the genuinely new future. However, as Jacob Jervell's careful study of St. Paul makes clear, the *Endzeit gleich Urzeit* formula cannot be considered as an accurate description of his theology of history.[35] To the extent that the pattern is discernible in Paul, it is there as a typological model or vehicle of expression which, for the most part, serves to remind us that Paul sees creation and salvation as the continuous work of God.

This conclusion in strengthened by the evidence Roy Harrisville assembled years ago concerning the New Testament view of history. Harrisville's entire study points to the fact that novelty or newness is an essential feature of the kerygma. He challenges the *Urzeit-*

Endzeit theory of the cyclical interpretation of history made famous by Gunkel. Gunkel contended that the Babylonian Tiamat-Marduk myth, which describes events in *arch-time,* passed into Jewish and then Christian hands (as evidenced in Revelation 12, 13, 17, and 21). Both Judaism and Christianity transformed it into an *Endzeit* description, eliminating polytheistic elements. Thus, in Revelation the things described of the *Urzeit* will characterize the *Endzeit*—a recapitulation of all things; the second creation is considered entirely after the analogy of the first. Gunkel further contended that a great many Christian doctrines such as the old man and new man, Christology, predestination, and the original condition before the Fall reflect this form of the equation of the last with the first. Harrisville counters by pointing out that Gunkel was driven to his conclusion because he attributed the cyclical view of history characteristic of Babylonian nature religion (which allows for no novelty in history) to the biblical writers. But such is not the case. The Bible sees history in linear terms, moving toward an ultimate conclusion.[36]

> The biblical concept of time cannot be conceived of in cyclic terms, but in linear terms, in terms of a continuous movement in which God ever more clearly discloses his will to men and thus draws history on to its appointed close.[37]

Moreover, Gunkel has disregarded the incarnation and its importance within the framework of history. The New Testament authors regard it as something totally new which gives history an entirely new direction.[38]

Wolfhart Pannenberg, following Brevard Childs, adds yet another dimension to this matter of *Urzeit* and *Endzeit*. The Old Testament gives evidence that Israel "demythologized" the cyclical thinking of mythical materials by directing their understanding of reality toward "an eschatological future rather than a primal and archtypal period of the past."[39] The thesis of Gunkel is therefore inadequate. Still, it is also not totally accurate to say that the linear view of time associated with salvation history simply replaced the cyclical view of myth. Jewish and Christian eschatology literature does "express the idea that the final age and the primal age *correspond.*" However, the correspondence should be understood typologically. Primordial themes of creation and paradise as well as historical events of salvation provide the types for giving expression to a future which fulfills, surpasses, and perfects the hopes and promises which the recollection of the type projects.[40] Thus, "typological analogy makes possible a consciousness of the future which has a definite content, notwithstanding its complete novelty."[41] It is this openness to the future and the concomitant element of historical novelty that distinguish the typological from the mythological mode of thought. And it is the typological interpretation of eschatology that enabled primitive Christianity to see in Jesus and his resurrection the inauguration of the events of the end which Jewish faith had anticipated.[42]

The foregoing discussion suggests to me that the strong eschatological orientation of the image sayings in the Bible justifies their further interpretation in the larger framework of the eschatological theology traced in the previous chapter. Therefore, I think we are ready to attempt an eschatological doctrine of the image of God. Indeed, on the basis of the discussion of this final section, I believe we can draw a conclusion that anticipates this reconstruction in part.

In terms of the biblical view of history, the eschatological realization of the new creation in Christ is not a recovery of the original; it is the fulfillment of it. As such, *Endzeit* is in a real sense prior to *Urzeit*. The future is prior to the past as the whole transcends the parts. *Endzeit* is anticipated in *Urzeit* and, as radically new, in its overcoming of the deleterious effects of sin and evil, *Endzeit* surpasses it. In terms of our concern with the image, we can say that, as the Old Testament understood its creation theology in light of a prior salvation theology, so we realize that it is only in the revelation of Christ and the promise of our humanity being fulfilled in him that we understand fully that this destiny has constituted our humanity from the beginning.

Chapter VII

Eschatological Man

What I intend in the following discussion of eschatological man is a statement of the doctrine of the image of God which will gather up the substantive insights of the history of Christian thought and biblical study and restate them in the framework of the often neglected eschatological orientation of Scripture in general and the image concept in particular. In the process of doing this, I also want to suggest, at least briefly, how this perspective on man correlates with the sense of temporality, becoming, and futurity that pervades our contemporary outlook on man and reality. I shall make this attempt on the basis of four theses on the image of God, the last of which serves as a bridge to the final part of this study.

> Thesis I: *The image of God refers to the distinctive way in which man's whole being as personal and historical being reflects God's being as personal and historical being.*

The biblical evidence we have reviewed indicates that the image of God is a concept referring to the whole of man's being. We cannot think of him as image in an overly spiritualized sense or in an overly material sense. He is the unity of both. As image of God, man is created for a special, distinctive relationship of immediacy to God. Yet man as image is only image; he is created theomorphically and therefore reflects and represents the being of God even as his dominion over the earth is but a representational one. Therefore, his being in the image is decidedly dependent being, despite its distinctiveness. It is possible to say that, as a measure of his distinctive communion with God, man ultimately finds the fulfillment of his nature and destiny in no one save God himself. It is constitutive of his being to live in close communion and union with God. Consequently, the image concept entails the idea of personhood as the necessary basis of this relationship. This, of course, correlates with the biblical vision of God as a personal God who relates himself to men.

Despite those instances in the history of Christian thought where the image has been defined in terms of ontic qualities such as reason and freedom or divided in terms of spiritual and natural dimension, there have been those who have captured the essentials of the biblical view. This is particularly true of thinkers like Augustine and Tillich but it is also true of the Reformation understanding of the image as original righteousness. This concreated righteousness is a state of affairs in which man is in perfect communion with God; he grasps and reflects the divine, and his will is at one with God's.

The first thesis I have stated comprehends these long-established insights of the tradition but it also goes beyond traditional formulations in expressly stating that the personal being of the image and of God whose likeness it is is historical being. That the being of God can be conceived in historical terms has already been developed by the eschatological theology we briefly reviewed. That is, we understand the structure of historical existence to be determined by the pattern of God's activity in promise and fulfillment. God is the bearer of history, and the eschatological future he promises and proleptically reveals in the Christ is that which gives meaning to the whole of history. It is the projection of the horizon of universal history. From this perspective we are led to the conclusion that history is the locus of God's revelation of himself. And, since we must understand history from the standpoint of its future, we are led to the further conclusion that the future is the *prius* of reality. It is ontologically prior to the past and the present. The kingdom of God is the biblical symbol for this coming future.

The idea of an historical understanding of God is, then, further developed by Pannenberg's explanation of his crucial point that God's being cannot be conceived apart from his rule. God's rule from the standpoint of the eschatological vision of reality is most aptly described as the power of the future. However, in stating this, one does not simply speak of God in terms of a future that is less concrete than a more real past and present. The reality of the future is present in the concrete way in which God is present in history to draw past and present creatively toward their fulfillment in the future. This is what makes our understanding of the significance of

Jesus' resurrection as the prolepsis of the future kingdom so important. In this we see the presence of God as the power of the future concretely manifest. It is also the appearance of the radically new in the midst of history. The possibility of such an occurrence of genuine novelty is a corollary of the additional insight that, as the power of the future, God operates with freedom in the contingency of events.

Rather than understanding reality as an ineluctable product of forces in the past which determine the future, we experience the future of our historical existence as possessing the ambivalence and indeterminacy of contingency. Our relationship to the future therefore has a personal character. That which is beyond control, that which is capable of the radically new which was only a vague possibility before, that which must therefore be approached with an attitude of trust rather than an attempt at predictability and control is that which is truly personal. This is the nature of the future when it is understood as creatively prior to the past. And from this perspective we are helped to see how God, as the power of the future, may be understood as personal being. That is, he may be so understood if the future displays unity as well as contingency. Even as the resurrection of Jesus becomes meaningful against the backdrop of apocalyptic hope for the future kingdom of God, new events must be related to a vision of the whole which gives them meaning by placing them within a unity that exceeds the dimensions of the event itself. Without this unity the contingency of the future would be experienced as pure chance. However, the revelation of the kingdom of God as the eschatological horizon of universal history provides the unity of the future within which we can understand contingent events in terms of the impact of that coming kingdom.[1] Consequently, when, within the context of the eschatological perspective of the Bible, we speak of God as "the power of the future," we use a phrase that comprehends his being as both historical and personal.

In speaking of God as the power of the future, Pannenberg feels compelled to speak in a qualified sense of the not-yet-realized nature of God's being as well:

> Jesus proclaimed the rule of God as a reality belonging to the future. This is the coming Kingdom. The idea was not new, being a conventional aspect of Jewish expectation. What was new was Jesus' understanding that God's claim on the world is to be viewed in

terms of his coming rule. Thus it is necessary to say that in a restricted but important sense, God does not yet exist. Since his rule
and his being are inseparable, God's being is still in the process of
coming to be. Considering this, God should not be mistaken for an
objectified being existing in its fullness. In this light, the current
criticism directed against the traditional theistic idea of God is quite
right.[2]

However, Pannenberg has not simply invented this notion of God's
coming to be to avoid the atheist criticism. He means here to express
the historicality of God's being as a corollary to the observable
phenomenon of reality as temporal process or emergence.

Given this account of divine historicality, we are better able to
understand God as the ground of human freedom and subjectivity.
The concept of God in traditional theism is at odds with the reality
of human freedom as the core of subjectivity or personhood. The
idea of God as *existent* being acting with omnipotence and omnis-
cience leads to a divine determinism that stands in conflict with our
experience of the contingency of history and the freedom of man.
The age-old dilemmas of providence and predestination illustrate
this conflict. Moreover, not only does the theistic view of God curtail
freedom and contingency, "but such a being would also not be God,
because it could not be the reality which determines everything, for
the reality of freedom, of human subjectivity would remain outside
its grasp."[3] The theistic notion of God as existent being is therefore
in conflict with the biblical idea of divine omnipotence. Furthermore,
it is far more appropriate for Christian theology to think of God as
the ground of freedom. This certainly accords with the biblical and
traditional understanding of man in the image of God as one who
possesses by virtue of that special creation the marks of freedom
in personhood for an immediate relationship with God.

In addition, speaking of God as the source of human freedom
picks up the Pauline and Johannine stress on freedom as a description of the outcome of God's atoning action. Understanding God in
terms of his historicality, his futurity as the coming God, enables
us better to understand him as the ground of freedom and, therefore,
to reflect more clearly the biblical idea of God. Freedom and
futurity belong together. Both concepts refer to the not-yet-realized.
Completely realized, existent being, without a future, does not fit
the idea of freedom in personality. Freedom is the core of subjectivity

or personality. God, in granting man a future in creation and redemption, is thus the source of human freedom and personality. God, in turn, in his own futurity is decidedly free and personal, as the Bible and Christian tradition have always maintained.[4] Once more, it is underscored that historicality and personality are corollaries in our understanding of the biblical idea of God.

Correspondingly, man's being in the image of God, as personal being derivative of and dependent upon God's personal being, is historical as well. Here the biblical evidence of the preceding chapter which uncovered the eschatological orientation of the *imago Dei* as a statement of promise and destiny is immediately relevant. Man's essential futurity and, therefore, historicality correspond to the priority of the future in an eschatological view of reality. Becoming man "images" the futurity of the coming God.

This understanding of man in terms of his futurity as a personal-historical being can be correlated with a number of models for the nature of human existence that have arisen in modern thought. Pannenberg for his part has entered into dialogue with modern anthropology, particularly through the work of Arnold Gehlen. In his book *What Is Man?* Pannenberg observes that man is distinct from the rest of creation in "having a world." He is able to transcend his environment and shape it into a world through the creation of material and spiritual culture. These capacities lead man to ask beyond every horizon of achievement he has been able to attain. In his creative imagination he projects beyond all points to which he has come in his striving. He is open to the future, and his striving in openness is in the nature of a *drive,* an irrepressible impulse. Because drives indicate *dependencies,* and because man in his transcendent openness cannot find the satisfaction of his drive in finite realities, it is possible to describe his situation as *infinitely dependent.* This is the source of the religious life. To be open to the future in seeking and shaping a world is ultimately to be open to God the infinite, for only communion with God can provide that fulfillment which is beyond every horizon of the world and which encompasses and gives unity to that world.

Furthermore, man's openness to the future ultimately entails a hope beyond death. Without a hope of unity with God that includes life beyond death, man's openness and the restless striving that characterizes it are turned back upon themselves, resulting in frustration and despair.[5] Such a consequence serves to underscore man's infinite dependency and our previous observation that the biblical view of the image makes clear that man cannot find his fulfillment in the finite world or in his own accomplishments but, rather, only in communion and union with God. Moreover, the phenomenon of human futurity corresponds to the eschatological view of the image as man's ultimate destiny for union with God beyond death, a destiny which is the source of the freedom and personhood implicit in the phenomenon of human futurity.

For Pannenberg and Moltmann both, a further contribution to the ontological grounding of the theology of the future is provided by the metaphysic of the German Marxist Ernst Bloch. Bloch offers an ontology of the future, a philosophy of *"das Noch-Nicht-Seins."* Reality is a sea of possibilities; it is open to the advent of the new. Indeed, reality ought to be understood from the perspective of the expectation of the radically new from the future of possibility. The future is the open space out in front of the present which draws the present to itself. This is an ontology of process and becoming. It is correlated subjectively with the phenomenon of hope in the makeup of man. His daydreams, his will to utopia, his sense of anticipation and expectation, all bear witness to the subjective apprehension of the futurity of reality. It is an orientation toward the world that finds expression in the drive toward revolutionary change.[6]

Bloch's ontology offers an outlook on the history of the world and the self that stands in contrast to a mechanistic concept of reality in which all things are ultimately determined by ineluctable forces operating upon man and his communities.[7] It must also be distinguished from a metaphysic of emergence or from a cyclical renewal concept of history in which the hope for the self is in the recovery of the lost.[8] No, for Bloch the future-oriented process that is reality unfolds in the drive of the self for realization in the *telos* of the commonwealth of freedom. The self that is meant to be is there in the inner man at all times and is realized when inner becomes outer and is actualized. However, the pattern here is not a simple realization of past hidden potentials. The controlling force of realization is the *novum*. It is the new of the future that draws out the potential of the self.[9] Though subject to critical revision from the side of theology, Bloch's ontology of the priority of the future is an important point of contact for the eschatological perspective and contemporary thought on reality. Indeed, one might say that Bloch's vision shares the dynamic of Jewish and Christian eschatology in its approach to understanding history and human existence, a claim amply evidenced by Bloch's frequent appropriation of the language of biblical messianism and apocalyptic hope.

These and other evidences[10] that might be cited from the literature of modern reflection on anthropology serve to increase the apologetic value of redefining the image of God in eschatological terms. The fact that man experiences the ontological priority of the future in his own futurity means that he experiences an essential relatedness to God, who is the power of the future. This experience of relatedness is constitutive of his being as the image. It offers the "point of contact" for the Christian kerygma. As Pannenberg points out:

> . . . [One] can remain a theologian only if he takes up again the question that has already been abandoned, of the relationship of man to God which is already assumed by Christian faith, and of which it always has a prior consciousness in some form or another. Only if man, even outside the Christian message, is related in his being as man to the reality of God on which the message is based can fellowship with Jesus mean salvation to him. But if, even outside the Christian message, man already has a relationship with God whom the message of Jesus presupposes, then man must always have had, in some form, consciousness of this relationship which constitutes his being as man. For a creature endowed with self-consciousness may be mistaken about what makes him himself but he cannot simply remain unaware of it.[11]

The essential relationship of man to God that we are describing here under this first thesis on the image of God really indicates that the image of God represents an ontological communion with God. As such, it is another way of expressing the insight we have already met in Augustine's view of the image as the "restless" rational soul and in Tillich's notion of the image as a reflection of the *logos* structure of reality. Both thinkers see man's being in the image of God as the *a priori* of his being. In Augustine the image as rational soul is that aspect of man's makeup that enables him to apprehend God who, as the creative ground of being in *amor,* offers an immediate experience of the divine in everything, especially the soul. In Tillich man is the image of God because the ontological elements are

present in him on creaturely basis even as they are in the divine
ground of all being. That is, the *logos* structure of man is analogous
to the *logos* structure of God, and, therefore, he experiences the
immediate presence of the divine or the ultimate.

We have, then, in this first thesis the beginning of a new version of
"theonomous man," one that is based on an historical ontology of
the future. As such, it participates in overcoming the structural
dualities that we have seen in the achievement of both Augustine and
Tillich. However, it goes beyond this to suggest that the eschatological
perspective at the heart of this outlook also contributes to the overcoming of the duality of history and eternity, the discontinuity
between nature and destiny. For, in a real sense, the personhood
in both God and man that is the basis of the image is a function
of the historicality of futurity, and the fulfillment of man as the
image of God in the arrival of the future is an event of the fulfillment
of universal history. This statement leads us directly into the next
thesis.

Thesis II: *The image of God is an eschatological concept which
refers to man's "destiny" for the fulfillment of perfect communion and union with God. The becoming of man in the
promise of this destiny is constitutive of his being.*

I have already said a great deal about the personal-relational nature
of the *imago Dei* both in the chapter dealing with biblical materials
and in the exposition of the previous thesis. I have also called attention to the historical-eschatological nature of the image concept. It
is clear in the New Testament that the image in its fulfillment is a
hope for the eschaton when our unity with God in Christ, who is *the*
image of God, will be complete in the resurrection of the dead and
the arrival of the kingdom of God. This indicates that the image is a
statement of "promise" and "destiny." Even the Old Testament is
susceptible to this interpretation as opposed to regarding the image
there as a purely protological construct. This means that perfect
communion and union with God, which a considerable segment of
the tradition described as the *justitia originalis* or the unimpaired
possession of the *donum superadditum* in the primordial state of
integrity, are something that belongs to the future of the fulfillment

of God's purpose in the consummation of his rule. This destiny is the gift of God's creation of man. Several conclusions follow.

In the first place, we are seeing man's being here in terms of its futurity as "not yet" even as we have seen God's being in terms of its futurity. This does not mean, however, that man is not yet image of God in the present any more than God is "not yet" in the sense of still coming to be. God is present to every present as its future. Inasmuch as man is the image of God, we must say that he is that image in every present of human history because, in every present, the image is present to him as his future. This is in accordance with the ontological priority of the future and the historical-eschatological nature of man as personal being. In the end we shall know that we have always been image of God. Indeed, we see in the Christ, as true image of God, the proleptic revelation of that end fulfillment of the image which has constituted our destiny and our human existence from the beginning.

From this standpoint we view our origin as from the future, the creation of the coming God whose kingdom is the future of the world. In a subsection entitled, "The Future Creates Past and Present," Pannenberg puts the matter in the following way:

> If the future of all creatures is a universal one, that is, if each instance of reality has the same future, then the future to which I look forward today is the same future that confronted every earlier present. . . . Thus I come to view past events as having eventuated from the same future to which I look forward. And, of course, those past events were the finite future of yet earlier events. The past is related in this way to the power of the future to which I look forward at present. Only in this way can I remember the past with gratitude or sorrow, knowing that past events did not occur as matters of inexorable fact but occurred contingently. And so we can now understand even our past as the creation of the coming of God.[12]

In effect, this notion of the future as the source of our creation in the past is but a corollary of the combined ideas of the ontological priority of the future, the kingdom of God as the horizon of universal history, and the perspective of the future as the new paradigm of transcendence. "In the message of Jesus, creation and the eschatological future belong together."[13]

In the second place, what is already apparent must now be spelled out: we cannot construe the biblical account of paradise and Fall in the sort of way that conduces to a return-to-origins eschatology that depreciates the value of history. This results whenever we gear Christian anthropology to a primordial state in which man possessed the image in perfection and fullness but lost it subsequently to the fall into sin. This protological approach to anthropology reduces eschatological hope to a restoration motif, blunts our sense of the arrival of the genuinely new in the kingdom of God, and leaves us to view history as an essentially meaningless ebb and flow of events in a fallen world on the way to destruction. Rather, in maintaining a future-oriented doctrine of man, I would fasten onto certain aspects of the biblical studies. To begin with, we have seen that it is not at all certain that one can describe the biblical account of paradise as representing a state of perfection and original righteousness in the manner in which it was so interpreted by Augustine, Luther, and later Calvin. Indeed, there is evidence that in the early church such perfections were not accorded to paradise man. Irenaeus is a case in point in that he saw the first man as childlike. Furthermore, in the light of modern biblical scholarship, systematicians like Emil Brunner and Reinhold Niebuhr have backed away from a literal-historical version of paradise and Fall and have attempted to speak of paradise lost as a transhistorical phenomenon present to every man. Paul Tillich has described man before the Fall as being in a state of dreaming innocence.

The idea that man is revealed fully not at his origin but only in his eschaton is at stake here, and it is an idea that is not totally alien to the tradition, even in areas where one might expect the opposite. There was, for example, in Irenaeus the concept of "growth" which, as Wingren has endeavored to show us, indicated on his part a belief that man's full maturity as man was an eschatological hope. Georges Florovsky has pointed out that, despite strong impulses toward a cyclical, restoration eschatology, the Greek Fathers placed more emphasis upon the idea of eschatology as new creation.[14] His point is supported at least in part by Panagiotis Bratsiotis's observation that Gregory of Nyssa did indeed conceive of the possibility that the believers' union with Christ would ultimately lead to a state of being higher than man's original state.[15] We also recall from the discussion of Luther in Chapter Two that in his teaching on the image there was a sense in which he believed that man possessed the image only in hope. In his commentary of Genesis, Luther indicates that, even had Adam not fallen into sin, he was still destined for further development and perfection!

Beyond this, we must also recall that the Bible gives us no indication that the image was lost in the Fall. The evidence is really more to the contrary. Moreover, the understanding of the image as a special and immediate relationship to the divine, which is the gift of God, indicates, as has been pointed out, that the image is not ultimately something which man *possesses* and can therefore lose. Since man's being is constituted by this essential relatedness to God, he can never escape the image no matter how much at odds with his constitution sin may render him. To lose the image would entail that man has become essentially inhuman and totally incapable of hearing the Word as either law or gospel. A number of thinkers in the history of Christian thought have, of course, perceived the matter in this fashion. We would call for support in this viewpoint from Augustine, Tillich, Niebuhr, and Barth in particular. Even those such as Irenaeus, Aquinas, Luther, Calvin, and Brunner, who taught some notion of a loss of the image, were ultimately forced into a companion notion stating how at least a part of the image was not lost; some remainder had to be posited in order that man might yet be man.

The combined result of these conclusions is to obviate the structural dualisms which arise out of having to speak of man in terms of having lost all or a part of the image that he possessed fully at his origin and to eliminate the mythical, ahistorical return-to-origins eschatology which forces a dualism of understanding human existence as a dichotomy between man's historical nature and his suprahistorical destiny.

It is important that we observe at this point that the position I have tried to develop here is also to be distinguished from the kind of historical view of man expressed in evolutionary progressivist views of reality. We recall in this connection the progressivist eschatology of Schleiermacher and Ritschl and the criticism I attached to it as inculcating an undervalued doctrine of sin and a suppression of the transcendent in history and eschatology. These tendencies (particularly the latter of the two) have come to full flower in the secularizing theologies of our century. However, beyond this, the progressivist perspective represents a conformity of our understanding of the futurity of the image to the causal pattern of nature. This outlook makes the future a product of past events and forces; the future becomes an emergence of past potentials in new configurations. This is quite different from this thesis' notion of the proleptic structure of man and history under the rubric of the ontological priority of the future.

A progressivist or developmental view of reality makes it difficult to see the sense in which man can concretely understand himself in the present to be the image of God. In our formulation of the image, man always is the image in the real sense of its being present to him as his future in every moment of history and, therefore, as definitive of his being in every past and present of life. Man has, as the God whom he images has, "futurity as a quality of being."[16] Moreover, in contrast to the general tendencies of evolutionary idealism, the present formulation of the image doctrine in terms of the priority of the future keeps faith with the biblical idea of creation and new creation as solely the product of God's divine action and, as such, the arrival of the genuinely "new," as Moltmann would stress it, *"ex nihilo."* From the beginning man's destiny for an intimate communion and union with God is in creation and redemption purely *sola gratia.* Man is only the image of God; his glory is a reflected glory.

> **Thesis III:** *From the perspective of law, the relationship of man's fallenness to his creation in the image of God should be understood as man's rebellion against his own destiny. From the perspective of gospel, man's hope for fulfillment in the image should be understood in terms of God's gracious determination, proleptically revealed in Christ, to fulfill the promise of man's creation in the divine image.*

I have already discussed the departure from the traditional notion of sin in terms of a fall from a primordial state of integrity accompanied by a loss of all or part of the image of God. However, we have also discussed the biblical view of the universal reality of man's sinfulness which the Fall narrative expresses. We can recall in this connection von Rad's remark that the Fall clearly conveys the idea that man has stepped outside his role as creature by choosing to follow his own will in opposition to God's. Man is therefore at odds with his own essential being in the image of God. This truth which we comprehend in the biblical idea of sin not only accords with Scripture but also, obviously, with human experience. Indeed, the impulse to hope, as we saw in Moltmann particularly, arises out of the keen sensitivity to the disparity between what we are and what we ought to be and were meant to be. The kingdom of God stands over against the evil of the present as a judgment and as a force that seeks, as Tillich might put it, to negate the negativities. As such the eschatological kingdom stands over against us as law and gospel; as judgment upon our lack and as a promise for our fullness.

In the light of these observations, it follows that the image of God as an expression of our eschatological destiny also stands over against us as both law and gospel. Our abiding essential relatedness to God which makes up the image is a constant evidence of the law written on our hearts. As a reproach built into our very nature, it makes the address of the Word as law all too understandable. This is so because the image remains to us as our future in every present of life and, because it does abide in that fashion, we can speak of sin as a rebellion against our own destiny, our own being. This constant combat characterizes every present of life, a resistance to the communion with God that is our ever present future. This conflict reflects the portrait of the sinful man divided against himself which St. Paul paints for us in Rom 7:15ff. In terms of the distinctive emphases of the theology of the future, rebellion against the image is essentially the refusal to be open to God's future and to the change it promises. It is genuine enmity on man's part because, ironically, it is this gracious future of communion with God that makes man the "person" he is with the freedom to choose rebellion.[17]

Man's rebellion against the image, as a resistance to God's future, echoes the Reformation understanding of sin as unfaith. The future as the arrival of the coming kingdom of God, as the presence of God who is the power of the future, is eminently personal, as I have tried to point out in discussing the first thesis. The infinite future of God is something we cannot encompass or control. Its personal and infinite character means that we can relate to it only in trust or faith. However, this essential relationship to God as our future, which belongs to our humanity as image of God, becomes perverted and sinful when man chooses self-trust for the sake of security instead of living in the trust of faith. When our relationship with other persons is marked by a desire to control and manipulate them instead of loving them, trusting them, and respecting their personal freedom and individuality, then those relationships have become perverted. So also, when we seek to gain control over God religiously or when we choose to place our trust in ourselves and in finite and controllable things, we deny God and are guilty of the root sin of unfaith.[18] Again there is irony for it is the blessing of the image that becomes the source of man's self-deception when he presumes that he can secure his destiny through dominance over the finite world. The abiding presence of that image is a judgment against such self-deception, however. Thus, even though I have defined the image in somewhat different terms, it is clear from this discussion of sin that the Reformers had a profound and true insight in speaking of sin as a loss of the image of God. This radical statement is appropriate in its force, for the image is man's essential center, and sin is a radical perversion of that center.

At the same time, as the kingdom of God stands over against us as the promise of the gospel, so also the image of God, as a statement of our eschatological destiny for life with God, has the nature of promise as well. In the Bible the image is clearly an eschatological hope for the kingdom of God, a hope to be fulfilled in the resurrection to perfect unity with God in Christ. Given this eschatological definition of the image, the resurrection of Jesus, as the prolepsis of the kingdom, is also the prolepsis of our humanity as fulfilled in the image of God. Notwithstanding the fact that the interest of the New Testament texts is in *eikon* as a divine predicate of Christ, we may say that the Christ is the *eikon tou Theou* in the sense of true humanity as well. If the fulfillment of our humanity as image of God is realized in the resurrection victory of the kingdom of God, then the resurrection of Jesus as a real man must also be the revelation of true, eschatological *imago*-humanity, the prolepsis of our prototype. In his person Jesus presents to man that reality in which he may share by the grace which Jesus himself has brought in through his atoning action. It is a gift that fulfills the deepest longings of the human condition, alienated as it is from its own true being as the image of God.

In Jesus, as the prolepsis of our true humanity, we have the gospel revelation that God is determined to bring to fulfillment his creative intentions for man despite man's resistance to his own nature as destined for God. In Jesus, the Christ, we are presented with the grace of God who is the power of the future. The salvation which the Christ event confers is the impact of that power of the future upon our human present. The power of the future, as we have said, is the source of human freedom. It liberates man from his present existence which is broken and regressive in order to free him for his future of authentic human existence revealed in Christ. The Christ event, therefore, represents the power of the future in contradiction to the destructive forces to the end that human destiny might be fulfilled in perfect communion and union with God. If we see this in connection with our observations in the previous thesis that creation is from the future, in terms of the power of the future as the force determining every past within the horizon of the universal future of the kingdom, then we can see in this context that the prolepsis of the future kingdom in Jesus is an act of God's creation. This accords with the Pauline emphasis that the hope for eschatological fulfillment in the image is hope in a "new creation" brought about by Christ in his resurrection victory and consummated in our resurrection. Eschatology, ktisiology, and soteriology belong together as intimately related.

Thesis IV: *An eschatological doctrine of the image of God provides us with a significant locus for the theological foundations of the Christian ethic.*

In dealing with the New Testament materials in particular, we have seen that Jesus as the *eikon tou Theou* is our prototype in two senses. He is our prototype of true *imago*-humanity in the sense I have just discussed by speaking of Jesus as the prolepsis of our humanity in revealing its eschatological fulfillment through perfect union with God in the resurrection. It is the additional sense in which Jesus is our prototype for the Christian way of life that now requires further development. In Phil. 2:5ff. we observed that Jesus' self-emptying love is the example for the Christian life. In contrast to the first Adam, who sought to reach beyond his dependent status as only "image" of the God, the last Adam, who is *the* image of God in his divine dignity, willingly emptied himself to suffer for the many. Even as the hope for the fulfillment of our humanity is also stated in this text via the reference to Christ's victory and exaltation that follows the statement concerning his kenosis, so also the nature of our true humanity as men who live in that hope is to be understood in terms of his self-giving love. This is the life-style of the person who is created anew in the image of God.

The Christian is raised and exalted with Christ through baptism. This baptism in Christ to a new creation is a renewal after the image of God—after Christ who is *the* image of God. These ideas emerge in both Col. 3:9–11 and Eph. 2:22–24 where the focus is the transformation of the believer according to the image of God in Christ. In the former text the immediate context is parenetic material concerning the way of the new life of the Christian (3:1–17). The larger context, particularly 2:11ff., concerns the dying and rising with Christ to new life in baptism. This dying and rising with Christ to new life are the basis of the ethic of the Christian (3:1–3) who is now to "seek the things that are above" (v. 1). That being the case, the Christian is to put on the new man and put off the old man whose sins are the sins of the flesh (vv. 5 and 8). The new man, characterized by his way of life (vv. 12ff.), is one whose nature is "being renewed in knowledge after the image of its creator" (v. 10) in Christ through baptism.[19] In Eph. 4:22–24 we have a parallel saying in which the new creation after the image of God emerges as the clear basis for the Christian life of putting off the old nature and its corruption and putting on the new. This new creation mediated by baptism is the motive force for an ethic of love patterned after Christ, the prototype.

The new humanity of the image of God in Christ stands, once more, in contrast to the old humanity typified by Adam. Putting off the old nature and putting on the new means that one's way of life is characterized by the qualities of God's love which Christ reveals as the divine image. Therefore, in both his destiny and demeanor the believer bears the divine likeness. The edifice of the Christian's life, mediated as it is by baptism and energized by the indwelling of the Spirit, is built upon the foundation of God's grace in Christ. Because grace is at the root of the Christian ethic, the indicative forms the basis of the imperative. Again, both Col. 3:9–11 and Eph.

4:17–24 present the same pattern: the imperative of putting on the new nature and putting off the old is comprehended in the indicative of being newly created in the image of God in Christ through the grace of baptism.

The eschatological thrust of the image saying here enables us to amplify these basic thoughts in terms of our own peculiar perspective of the future. The new man created anew and transformed after the image of God in Christ has been redeemed by grace from the sin which stands in opposition to the eschatological destiny as image of God which constitutes his humanity. This new creation in Christ is in continuity, therefore, with God's creating action at man's origin. Here in Christ, as in the beginning, the image is given as a creation "*ex nihilo*"; that is, as a pure gift of grace that comes from the power of the future as the arrival of the radically "new." In view of this one can say that man is given in Christ the future of his fulfillment. Having this future he is freed for the values of the kingdom by being freed from his own drives to secure his own future in terms of the finite realities he can control: he is freed from the fundamental sin of rejecting his creaturehood and dependency as *imago Dei*. When he is freed in this way by the indicative of God's grace, the overarching imperative of the Christian ethic from our own futurist perspective is "Become what you will be!"[20]

The dynamic and criterion of this imperative is love, the *agape* love revealed in *the* image of God, our prototype, Jesus Christ. The image notion therefore includes not only our intimate communion and union with God in a relationship of mutual love but the love of our neighbor as well. Karl Barth's teaching concerning the image is perhaps the strongest in the tradition on this point. Barth bases this horizontal dimension of the image as involving love for the fellowman upon the fact that man was created in the image as male and female. It is in analogy with this primordial and most intimate of human relationships that Barth can assert that the image entails a similar relationship and disposition of love with the fellowman.[21] Barth's exegesis on this point appears strained but his instincts are correct. From the standpoint of Jesus as our prototype in being the image of God both as true God and as true man, we can also conclude that the perfect love for the other which comes to expression in him is also to be included in the image concept along with love for God.

Jesus' unity with the Father and his unity with mankind are thus two sides of the same image notion.[22]

The *agape* love of Jesus our prototype is the dynamic by which Christians are related to the world in seeking the kingdom of God. In seeking the kingdom, *agape* seeks the unity of God and man and man and man displayed by the Christ as the prolepsis of the kingdom. Indeed, the unity of all men is a corollary of the unity of man with God which is integral to the *imago Dei,* for this unity of all men corresponds to the universality of the one God in unity with whom we were all created as image of God. In the service of this unity, love seeks the values of life, freedom, equality, peace, harmony, and joy for the fulfillment of the individual and the whole community of humankind. These are the eschatological values revealed in the Christ as a further statement of the nature of that perfect unity of God and man and man and man that is the heart of his prolepsis of the kingdom of God and true humanity. The Christian, who is in Christ, participates proleptically in the final destiny that these values describe. As one thus in Christ, the Christian is an ambassador of God's future kingdom, and his efforts to seek its values for all mankind are a continuance of the prolepsis given in Christ. To be sure, the extent to which these values may be attained in history this side of the kingdom is only fragmentary and penultimate. However, even the fragmentary realization of such value is a preliminary manifestation of the ultimate and, as an intuition of the ultimate, is to be cherished both as a preparation for the kingdom's arrival and as a proleptic witness to the present impact of its coming for faith and for hope.[23]

The values of the kingdom, as expressions of the eschatological ultimate, have the force of absolutes. They stand over against us as law and gospel, even as the kingdom is both judgment and promise in being the universal horizon of God's future which confronts every historical present. The values of the kingdom as concrete words spoken against the way of the sinful world summon up the dualism that cannot be explained away, the dualism that exists in the contrast between the kingdom and the fallen world. However, this dimension of law stands in correlation with the dimension of gospel. These values of the kingdom are concrete expressions of the fulfillment of our humanity in the image of God, which God intended from the beginning of creation and has secured by the grace of Christ in the new creation. *In that this fulfillment is the completion and determining future of our historical existence as created in and for the* imago Dei, *we see in the eschatological promise of the image and the values associated with it a continuity between man's nature and destiny.* It is finally this continuity, which is built upon the gospel as an extension of God's creative action, that we have been seeking all along.

Part Three

Eschatology and Ethics

Chapter VIII

Grounding the Good

My task now is to indicate in what ways the eschatological reconstruction of the doctrine of man can contribute to the foundations of the Christian ethic. We shall see that the dualisms observed in the history of Christian anthropology have an effect upon our interpretation of the foundations of the Christian ethic and pose problems for the construction of its normative theory. The mitigation of the dualisms in the history of the *imago* doctrine, which the eschatological perspective has helped to bring about, will prove helpful in resolving some of the dilemmas in ethical theory as well.

These final chapters deal with the two basic questions of normative ethics: "What is the good?" and "What is the right?" A bridge from the constructive theological efforts previously discussed to the questions of normative ethics was built by the previous chapter. There I tried to demonstrate that the image doctrine is an appropriate locus for the discussion of the theological foundations of the Christian ethic. The relevance of the eschatological perspective to the ethical task was at least implicit. However, before we address the first of these two ethical questions, it seems well to add a further word of transition concerning the relationship of eschatology and ethics.

THE RELATIONSHIP OF ESCHATOLOGY AND ETHICS

When we reflect for a moment upon the fact that Christian ethics is essentially a discipline derivative of systematic theological foundations, it is not surprising that the eschatological dimension should be so conspicuously absent in much of Christian ethics. Our brief analysis of the tradition concerning the *imago Dei*, as well as our discussion of the recent renaissance of apocalyptic study and the development of eschatological theology, has already shown that theology has frequently de-eschatologized history or dehistoricized eschatology. The ethicist has therefore had little encouragement for regarding eschatology as a key to the foundations of the Christian ethic. However, both Pannenberg and Moltmann have made important steps in relating the results of their theologies to the realm of ethics. This is a foundation on which we can build. Beyond this, other recent studies in both biblical and systematic theology have demonstrated the lively relationship of eschatology and ethics and have, thus, paved the way for my efforts here.

From the field of biblical studies the work of Richard Hiers calls for some special attention. Hiers has worked extensively on the eschatological concept of the kingdom of God.[1] He is consistent and persistent in asserting, as Weiss and Schweitzer had done before, that Jesus' thinking and teaching concerning faith and ethics are pervaded by his eschatological expectation of the imminent arrival of the kingdom of God. The Sermon on the Mount must indeed be understood as an "interim ethic," one that is radical in its demands because the time is short and the presence of the end is at hand. This imminent kingdom is the reality of all-surpassing importance for the message of Jesus. Only when this fact is grasped can the various injunctions of Jesus' ethical teachings be understood aright. Only when this eschatological perspective is kept uppermost can the truly radical nature of Jesus' sayings be safeguarded against reductionist or "spiritualized" interpretations which seek to present them in more palatable form.[2] However, notwithstanding the perennial problem that this conclusion creates for the validity of Jesus' ethic in light of the continuance of the age some twenty centuries hence, Hiers does not suggest that we seek some easy solution to extricate ourselves from the problem while still saving the ethic in some form or another. Indeed, he rejects all attempts to detach Jesus' ethics from his eschatology, to de-eschatologize his theology or to dehistoricize his eschatology.[3]

Hiers proposes essentially that we should embrace the eschatological dimension of Jesus' ethics not only as the most accurate reflection of the historical Jesus[4] but also as an abiding dimension of the nature of the Christian ethic that finds expression in at least two emphases. The first of these is that all Christian ethics must be understood in a sense as "interim" ethics. That is, the time is short. Eschatological ethics reminds us of the finitude of our lifetime and that of the others we are called to serve in love. In the face of human finitude and the coming kingdom, decision must be now. Secondly, eschatology is relevant to the Christian ethic in terms of hope. We no longer look for the kingdom of God as a result of an evolutionary development of human moral effort. The kingdom stands in judgment on such pretense and reminds us that the redemption of history must ultimately be a miracle of grace. At the same time, the symbols of the eschaton are such that they promise that God will redeem history and establish his reign. Therefore our actions in history, done in the name and under the impetus of his love, are meaningful actions. In sum, the eschatological vision is one of both judgment and promise for our historical existence. It allows for neither naive developmentalism nor other-worldly detachment from concern for the structures of history.[5] In the final analysis, it is the theology of hope, as developed by Pannenberg, Braaten, and others, that for Hiers promises to be the most appropriate systematic expression of the implications of Jesus' eschatological vision.[6]

Another study of significance for demonstrating the general relevance of eschatology for understanding the Christian ethic is a recent dissertation written for Wolfhart Pannenberg by Norman Metzler entitled "The Ethics of the Kingdom." Metzler's study deals with Ritschl's theology of the kingdom of God and Johannes Weiss's critique of the Ritschlian position from the standpoint of Jesus' apocalyptic-eschatological proclamation of the kingdom of God. This leads not only to the question of whether or not Ritschl's handling of the kingdom concept was justified but, more importantly and more generally, to the question of whether or not there is any close relationship between eschatology and ethics Ritschl affirmed their necessary connection. For him the kingdom was both divine gift and ethical task; it was the religious and ethical highest good.[7] In making this connection, Ritschl departed from the view expressed by traditional dogmatics, which maintained the heterogeneity of eschatology and ethics. The former was considered essentially religious and other-worldly, referring to the kingdom to be established at the end of time by God alone. The latter was seen as a worldly, human enterprise. Ritschl, for his part, veered more to the worldly side, stressing the priority of ethical striving in his developmental scheme of the gradual realization of the kingdom of God in history through the ethical self-realization of humankind.[8]

As is well known, Ritschl's scheme came under attack by both Johannes Weiss and Albert Schweitzer. They both discerned that Jesus' proclamation reflected the eschatological ideas of late Jewish apocalyptic. His ethic involved a rejection of all worldly goods and standards.[9] Obviously, these insights severely undermined Ritschl's eschatology. However, neither the Ritschlian school nor Weiss and Schweitzer themselves could accommodate these findings in a new theological construction. The question thus remains, can the historical understanding of the kingdom of God so strong in Ritschl be wedded to the eschatological understanding of the kingdom, which Weiss held Jesus taught, in such a way that the close relationship of eschatology to ethics (Ritschl's achievement) is demonstrated by seeing the kingdom of God as historical-eschatological rather than *either* historical *or* eschatological? As Metzler correctly observes, subsequent theological efforts have failed to embody this "Ritschl-Weiss" nexus. Indeed, the failure to overcome the traditional separation of history and eschatology and, therefore, the discontinuity of ethics and eschatology is reflective of the sort of dualism we have been struggling with throughout this study.

Metzler believes that Pannenberg's theology makes a great contribution to dealing with this problem. It is the proleptic character of the eschatological kingdom, as Pannenberg works it out, that affords the clue to how we can understand the kingdom of God as both a realistic-futuristic hope and a reality of history relevant to the ethical activity of historical existence. In language that reflects Pannenberg and supports the propositions of this study concerning the image of God, Metzler offers the following as an explanation of the significance of the proleptic character of the kingdom, first of all for historical existence in general:

> The meaning of this for human life in general is that man lives in hope for the final fulfillment of his ultimate destiny; he *anticipates* in his present life that vision which he entertains of his final destiny and true nature. For his true nature will only be realized and known in the final future of all things. . . .[10]

When it is further understood that this proleptically present kingdom of God is for Pannenberg, as it was for Ritschl, the highest good, then its significance for the Christian ethic can also be articulated. Christian ethical striving under the present impact of the coming kingdom becomes, in its quest for the highest good, an anticipation or proleptic representation of the kingdom of God. In this perspective Ritschl's joining of ethics and eschatology is maintained without sacrificing Weiss's insight that, for Jesus and the New Testament, the kingdom of God is a realistic future hope.[11]

In sum, by showing the intimate relationship of ethics and eschatology through their work on the kingdom of God concept, Hiers and Metzler help to set the stage for the remarks that follow on the relevance of an eschatological doctrine of the image of God for the foundations and theoretical structure of the Christian ethic.

THE THEOLOGICAL AND ONTOLOGICAL GROUNDING OF THE GOOD

As anyone who has studied Christian ethics is aware, there is a myriad of competing options concerning the appropriate normative theory for Christian ethics. The theological and ontological base of the Christian ethic must be clarified if we are to progress toward a greater resolution of the conflicts of choice that exist within Christian normative theory. But what shall be our starting point in this task? Does the question of the right or the question of the good take precedence? Wolfhart Pannenberg has suggested that the best starting point for ethical investigation is the "good." It is worthwhile to quote him at length on this point:

> That ethics has to do with what is beyond the presently realized human condition is not a peculiar insight of our modern era. It is to be discovered in the origins of classical philosophical ethics, in the Socratic doctrine of the good. There the good was identified as that which all people lack and for which they strive. As they strive for the good, they strive for what is good *for them*. Of course, people deceive themselves about what is good for them, but they strive for it. At least this is clear: the good is that which man does not yet possess conclusively, that which he must still strive to realize. The good contains in itself the difference between value and being. The good is "beyond being," Plato said. In speaking this way, Socrates and his followers were not deriving their ethics from arbitrary imperatives but from a structural description of human action. What they agreed upon in their discussion and what we can agree upon

today is that the structure of human action reveals a striving for the good. . . . The quest for the good, seeking what is good for human beings, still provides the best starting point for ethical investigation.[12]

To this we would add the reminder that love, both in its origin in God and in its appropriation as a way of life for the disciple, is creative of new life and the fulfillment of the *humanum*. It follows from this that the good toward which love strives must be known; that is, the first question for the Christian ethic must be "What is the fulfillment of the nature and destiny of man?" This is the question that has occupied the tradition in its treatment of the image of God concept, and it has been the burden of this study as well. As was made clear, the long history of theological reflection on the image of God never really displayed an instance where some form of fundamental dualism in the understanding of human existence was not present. This very dualism in the theological formulation of the *humanum* is reflected in the crucial question of ethics as to whether or not we ought to understand the fulfillment of man's being (the realization of the good) in terms of an other-worldly or this-worldly vision. This question has also failed to be answered with any consensus in the long tradition of Christian ethics. I would submit that the failure, in large measure, has been a product of the more fundamental problem we have dealt with in our attempt to address the dualities apparent in the history of the Christian doctrine of man.

For us to say that the good in terms of the fulfillment of the *humanum* as the goal of love is the prior question for Christian ethics is not to say that the love has no content for the moral life in and of itself. Indeed it does. One can say that in Christ, as love incarnate, we have a very concrete vision of the life of love revealed in his teaching, his passion, his self-giving, his equal regard for all men, and his devotion to the Father. One may also derive much content for the concept of *agape* love from 1 Corinthians 13: love is patient, kind, it is not selfish, it does not rejoice in the suffering of others, it is not jealous, etc. But in all this we are talking about an orientation to life, a disposition of the heart which is compelling and itself rooted in the experience of the creative love of God. The experience of love is faith's experience of the promise of life that frees us from fear and enables us to serve the good of others. This is just the point. Our notion of an ethic of love is not complete unless it is grounded in the *telos* toward which love drives. Our Lord is the prime case in point; the supreme love made manifest in him was love acting toward the fulfillment of a purpose: the revelation of God's *telos* for all mankind and for the universe.

The good toward which love strives is the fulfillment of man's created destiny in God, in Christ. If the vision of man's being and future which we may discern at the theological base of the Christian ethic is compelling—if we can give ontological grounding to this vision of the good—then the ethic of love will be vindicated and its substance more readily discerned. The question of the good is the best starting point. If one, Joseph Fletcher for example, fails to deal with the matter in the fashion that we have just indicated, we observe a love ethic of situationism without meaning as an ethical option for Christians. Fletcher refers to love as the only intrinsic value as though the concept of love is able to answer both the questions about the good and the right.[13] In his system, however, love remains the disposition of good will toward one's fellowman. There is no substance offered as to the *telos* of love and, therefore, love's actualization is left to the relativities of each situation and the intuition of the involved moral agent. The good is neither theologically nor ontologically grounded; it is transferred to the disposition of love exemplified by Jesus.

The theological and ontological grounding of the good obviously means that we seek an ethic that is rooted in a compelling universal vision of reality, an ethic that will arise out of a comprehensive statement of what we are, what we ought to be, and what we can hope for, a statement that commends itself because it somehow touches the depths of human experience in such a way that we are enabled to assent, to hope, and to act.

Philosophy has struggled continuously with the problem of whether the good is subjective or objective. The problem embodied in this debate is instructive. The advantage of the subjective view of value is that it relates the good to man and his needs and aspirations rather than simply presenting us with abstract ideas of the good which stand over against or above man as is the tendency of an objective theory. On the other hand, the objective theory of value avoids the radical relativity of a subjective theory which defines the good in terms of man's interest or satisfaction; it provides the element of transcendence which prevents us from deluding ourselves about man's actual state of affairs, and it enables us to make moral judgments, advise, praise, and blame.

The debate between subjective and objective theories of value is really in the same family as the perennial debate of absolutism versus relativism. It cannot be my purpose at this time to rehearse all the complex lines of this debate. However, in brief, the absolutist says that there are a good and a right in matters of moral concern that transcend the relativities of culture and the relativities of individual insights. By contrast the relativist begins by noting that moral judgments on the same matters are different from culture to culture, from subculture to subculture, and from one period of history to another. He then argues that what the situation is is what it ought to be. The absolutist's problem is that the notion of absolutes is difficult to sell to people in a pluralistic, tolerant modern world and cannot be demonstrated empirically. This is, conversely, the strength of the relativist argument. On the other hand, the relativist's problem is that his argument—ethical relativity exists; therefore, ethical relativism is true—is not logically sound; the middle term is missing. "Ought" cannot be derived from "is." However, more important than that, relativism gives no direction to the future of individuals or of societies, for conformity to what is current is substituted for ultimate meanings. There is no point from which to be critical and no goal toward which to aspire.

To bring together in harmony the truth of the subjective theory of the good and the objective theory of the good, to cope with the actuality of ethical relativity without losing the conviction of the absolute—these problems are all a piece of the primary problem of grounding our ethic in a universal understanding of reality that both offers a comprehensive vision of the ultimate and enables us to understand and concretely to cope with the relativities of our day-to-day experience of the world. The tension here is essentially identical with the tensions embodied in the dualities of nature and grace, nature and supernature, historical and suprahistorical, and physical and spiritual which have attached in various ways to the understanding of man in the image of God. The correlation of these dualities in theological anthropology with the dualities we have

been discussing here in Christian ethics is perhaps best justified if
we can demonstrate how the manner in which we attempted to
resolve the dualism in the doctrine of the *imago Dei* can provide a
similar service in the field of ethical theory.

In the Howison Lecture of 1954 at the University of California,
philosopher Brand Blanshard discussed the impasse that two
thousand years of ethical reflection has achieved in trying convincingly
to ground ethics in the good. His suggestion of a way out of this
impasse was to return to the vision of Plato that "the justification of
every act lays in its place in the form of the good life." He concludes:

> Goodness is dependent on the feeling and impulse of conscious
> minds. It consists in the satisfaction and fulfillment of human nature.
> Does this destroy the objectivity of our judgments of good and evil?
> On the contrary, it provides a clear meaning for their objective
> truth and frees that truth from any dependence on individual thought
> or feeling . . . to be moral is in the end to be natural and reasonable
> and sane.[14]

Thus, Blanshard attempts to bring together the subjective and objective views of the good by claiming that the very objectivity of moral
judgments is grounded in the fact that they arise out of the subjectivity of natural, reasonable man—there is, ultimately, no dichotomy of subjective and objective, of fact and value. For the theologian
the image that immediately leaps to mind is Luther's description of
the natural man as *in curvatus in se*. In the ethics of autonomy all
attempts to place the good on a footing other than the satisfaction
of human impulse are doomed to failure. There is here no way out of
eudaemonism. For the good, if it is to have objectivity, is intrinsic
good to be loved for its own sake and, if that good resides in the
subjectivity of man, the nature of its objectivity is self-love.

As a theologian, Pannenberg also feels that a return to Plato can
help us get our bearings in the business of giving ontological foundation to the good and therefore to ethics. However, his accounting of
Plato is fuller than that of Blanshard and his concern is quite the
opposite of attempting to ground the good in man alone:

> Plato's idea of the good had already, and not without good reason,
> been understood as his esoteric idea of God. If the good is to be
> distinguished from the happiness it grants, it must be something

within itself. Thus Plato spoke of the good as that which is beyond
being. The good then asserts an ontological priority over against
everything extant. The priority of the future over the present, which
is implied here, is of general relevance to metaphysics. If not only all
men but all things strive for the good, as in Plato's vision, we have
reason to think of the good as the divine that rules over everything.[15]

Here, of course, we see Pannenberg's understanding of Plato
emerging as a springboard into his own theology of the future.
But we must not get ahead of ourselves.

I have already pointed out that the concept of the fulfillment of
the *humanum*, as corresponding to the question of the good, has been
seen by some theologians more in other-worldly terms and by others
more in this-worldly terms. I also suggested that this polarity corresponds to the polarity between subjective and objective value
theories on the side of philosophy. If we opt for a subjective notion
of the good (or try to say that its objectivity resides in the subjectivity of man) then we have certainly opted for autonomous
ethics. But we have to sacrifice ultimately that transcendent element
of the good which enables us to make judgments from the standpoint
of that which is beyond the relativities of human existence. This is
finally the risk of stressing the this-worldly fulfillment of man as the
theory of the good for the ethics of love, as in the secularization of
the gospel. On the other hand, if we opt for the objectivity of the good
as standing over against man and as constituting his duty, we have
chosen heteronomous ethics. Even the philosopher who believes he
has arrived at a statement of the objective good solely by the path
of autonomous reason ironically finds himself plunged into heteronomy because, once the good has been named, it stands over against
the agent as intrinsic good, absolute, and, thus, in the same place
as a divine lawgiver. By the same token, if we choose in theology
to stress the fulfillment of man in an other-wordly sense we have
opted for heteronomy as well. In both cases we have lifted up the
element of transcendence but we risk sacrificing our sensitivity to
historical human need for the sake of transcendent suprahistorical
demand. In the theological context, life in this world as regards the
striving for the good in the midst of the relativities of history is
emptied of any genuine significance.

Neither autonomy nor heteronomy is totally adequate for the
grounding of our ethic. As we saw earlier, Tillich made this point

quite clearly in his attempts to offer instead the idea of theonomy as characteristic of the kingdom of God which stands beyond the contrast between heteronomy and autonomy. When the kingdom of God draws near under the conditions of history through the impact of the Spiritual Presence there is an unitive overcoming of the understanding of man in terms of a duality of this-worldliness and other-worldliness. This corresponds to what we discerned as Tillich's "theonomous" understanding of man in the image of God. The question of fulfillment of the good or human existence in the kingdom of God cannot be understood purely in this-worldly or other-wordly terms because man himself is not so divided. Rather man in his temporal reality as image of God is grounded in the divine ground of all being which at the same time transcends man. Nonetheless, we also recall that Tillich's scheme for relating the kingdom of God to the realities of historical existence was not wholly adequate because, in the final analysis, Tillich's eschatology was ahistorical. The real fulfillment of the *humanum* lies above history in eternal life, and the relationship of the kingdom of God to history is restricted to periodic, fragmentary attainments of theonomy as indicators of the permanent presence of eternal life. This does not bring us to a resolution of our problem of harmonizing the this-wordly and other-wordly aspects of human fulfillment in our attempt to give a universal grounding of the good.

Simply to pass by Tillich on this account would be a mistake however. Notwithstanding the final outcome of his theology, Tillich did after all evidence a vital social ethic that proceeded out of the center of his theology. His conception of the kingdom of God and the attendant notion of theonomy enabled him to bring the Ultimate immediately and meaningfully to bear upon man's striving for the good within the structure of temporal existence. This was perhaps best illustrated by the manner in which his theology led him to become an apologist for religious socialism in his early days in Germany. Two elements of his thought appear to be decisive for an understanding of how he was able to hold together in unity and tension the relative and absolute aspects of the good under the conditions of history. The first of these elements is the Protestant Principle, rooted in the doctrine of justification *sola gratia, sola fide*. This principle was a corollary of Tillich's conviction that existence is fallenness characterized by radical ambiguity. From the critical standpoint of the Protestant Principle Tillich could never say that life under the conditions of historical existence could ever achieve the fulfillment of its created destiny. Indeed, without grace nothing positive could be expected in this world. For this reason he stood over against the this-worldliness of the utopian and progressivist positions which erred in thinking that the kingdom, the ultimate, could ever arise out of the conditions of the finite.[16] In this he was true to the theology of the Reformation. On the other hand, his vision of the universal unity of all things in the divine ground, his ontology, led him to see all structures of existence as objects of grace. Thus, he could not rest with the sort of doctrine evidenced in some versions of the two kingdoms ethic where one had the salvation of individuals by grace with an ethic of love, on the one hand, and the ultimate damnation of historical structures with an ethic of law and power, on the other hand. Such a division of man's existence runs counter both to his theonomous vision of man and to the universal scope of grace which is a corollary of his ontology. Indeed, all structures of the universe, including sociopolitical institutions and other forms of culture, are open to the transforming impact of the Spiritual Presence. The this-worldly and other-worldly dualism of two realms of thinking could not be embraced.[17]

From the perspective of the Protestant Principle, then, Tillich was able to assert the relativity and fragmentary nature of all historical attainments of the good over against the optimism of utopian and progressivist autonomy and over against any pretense on the part of conservative pessimism to resist the necessity and possibility of continual transformation. From the perspective of the universal scope of grace as a corollary of his ontology he could assert the possibility of the meaningful—albeit fragmentary—attainment of the good within the structures of history over against the heteronomous view of Christian conservatism. In taking the theonomous path of the kingdom of God from the standpoint of the Protestant Principle and the universal vision of grace, Tillich provides us with a bridge to our current interest in the theology of the kingdom of God. If the kingdom of God can be rediscovered as a symbol of Christianity's universal vision of reality and grace without sacrificing its historicality on the one hand, and without capitulating to naive utopianism on the other hand, the best elements of Tillich's thought can be brought together in a new theonomy. An ethic built upon such a theonomous view of reality would presumably overcome the dichotomy between this-worldliness and other-worldliness in its understanding of the good without sacrificing the truth of either.

Pannenberg, as we noted earlier, has stated that the good is the best starting place for the ontological grounding of the Christian ethic. We also noted his affinity for Plato's thought in this connection. In the same article Pannenberg points out that Augustine's connection of the good with the divine was in continuity with the Platonic tradition, with certain exceptions due to Christian influence. In this respect, Augustine's Hellenism is an asset. However, in respect to the dualism that is associated with Platonic thought, Augustine's Hellenism also involves him in what Pannenberg considers the most serious defect in his ethics, a pessimism about this world which leads to what Pannenberg calls the "other-worldly distortion." This "other-worldly distortion" finds expression in terms of thinking about salvation as an escape from this world to life in another. Thus, Pannenberg:

> This escapism can be overcome only if we think of God differently. He is not a transcendent and self-sufficient being, caught in his own transcendence and separated from the world. Rather, he affirms the world relating to the world not only as its creator but as its future. All this is most sharply articulated in the idea of God as the One who is coming to establish his Kingdom in this world.
>
> The notion of the coming Kingdom of God complements the idea of the good. The idea of the good is essentially related to the present man and his world because the good is concerned with the future of this man and his world.[18]

In this notion of the good as connected with God in terms of the coming kingdom of God, the good is relative with respect to its present actualizations but absolute with respect to its essential futurity.

Pannenberg seeks to unite the this-worldly aspect of the good with the other-worldly or transcendent nature of good by gathering all historical reality together within the horizon of the coming eschatological kingdom of God. As in Tillich's thought, the transcendent element of the good prevents our fixing hope upon the finite structures of reality for a full realization of the good at any point in history: "This good has priority over against all human striving for the good." At the same time, all human action in seeking the good is granted meaningfulness within the horizon of the coming kingdom which is ultimately historical. Since God is not remote from us in transcendent self-isolation but the one who is coming in history, our faith in him and our commitment to him result in a *conversion to the world*:

> God is the ultimate good not in isolated transcendency but in the future of his Kingdom. This means that the striving for God as the ultimate good beyond the world is turned into concern for the world.
>
> This corresponds with God's intention for the transformation of the world through his rule. Such a reversal of the pious tendency of leaving the world behind for God's sake constitutes a *conversion to the world*. Here we see the exciting relevance of Jesus' message about the power of God's future upon the present. The most constructive consequence of this conversion to the world is the Christian idea of love that affirms the present world in transforming it.[19]

Thus, we see that the ethic of love is the dynamic which is actualized in its striving for the transformation of the world within the horizon of the coming kingdom of God. Vitalized by the hope that this future promise engenders, love seeks continually the realization of those values characteristic of the eschatological kingdom: life, peace, freedom, equality, unity, harmony, and joy. Here, then, we see in the association of the good with the concept of the future kingdom of God and with God as the power of that future both the theological and ontological grounding of the good. The kingdom as future reality, proleptically present, is the theological foundation of the good in being the new paradigm of transcendence appropriate to the eschatological perspective of the Bible. It is also an appropriate symbol for the ontological foundations of the good as well because it refers to the horizon of universal history which is the necessary ultimate for an ontology of the priority of the future.

It is within the framework of the theological and ontological grounding of the good, which eschatological theology provides, that I have developed an eschatological reconstruction of the image doctrine. The *imago* doctrine thus developed offers a sharper and more concrete focus for understanding the good within the context of an eschatological ethic. It answers the peculiar needs for a

Christian anthropology which I attempted to spell out in the very first chapter. Therefore, further statements about the nature of the good and eschatological ethics are based on the comments already made concerning eschatological theology in general and the *imago Dei* in particular.

THE IMAGE OF GOD AND THE GOOD

For the Christian ethic, the identification of the good is in the answer to the question of the fulfillment of man. The question of the fulfillment of the *humanum* leads us into Christian anthropology and our doctrine of the image of God. On the basis of what has already been said regarding the image of God, the first observation that follows is that the Christian ethic should be christologically based in a way that recalls much of the past tradition of christological ethics while yet offering a new insight. In the resurrection of Jesus of Nazareth, the Christ, we have the proleptic revelation of the kingdom of God. This same Christ is *the* image of God, the revealer of the divine in his victory and exaltation. At the same time, this proleptic revelation of the divine as a revelation of the future kingdom is also a prolepsis of our *imago*-humanity, our true humanity as image of God, which, by grace, is the created future destiny that is constitutive of our humanity in every present. The good as the fulfillment of the *humanum* is, thus, proleptically present to us in the Christ as the *eikon tou Theou*.

The good so revealed and grounded in the Christ as the prolepsis of the coming kingdom of God is absolute in virtue of its belonging to that eschatological future, which is the new paradigm of transcendence in an historical theology addressing a temporal view of reality. It is universal in scope as well, for the eschatological kingdom, to which the good as the fulfillment of the *humanum* belongs, is the theological corollary of universal history. Universal history, in turn, is the necessary outcome of the ontological priority of the future. The phenomenon of human futurity that we have briefly discussed lends credence to this notion of the ontological priority of the future. Furthermore, one of the phenomenological evidences for this futurity which we discussed under Thesis I in the previous chapter, the "natural" drive men have toward fulfillment in the universal horizon of the future (for theology, the kingdom of God), obviates strict relativism both inside and outside theological ethics. Relativism would have to deny the reality of that drive. At the same time, the future fulfillment of the good is proleptically revealed in Christ as the image of God to be that which is constitutive of all humanity in every present. This reality makes it possible to say further that the structure of human existence in the image of God is proleptic in nature and that the good is, therefore, evident in this structure as it has been opened up to us by the Christ. This observation also argues against relativism, for relativism can tolerate no such "essential" evidence of the good in the structures of existence.

This understanding of the good as revealed in our existence in the image of God constitutes a theonomous perception of the good. Because the good is disclosed in the *proleptic* nature of existence in the image, the good is neither a product of autonomy nor a product of heteronomy; it arises out of man's own being but only in the awareness that that being is dependent upon, derivative of, and "transparent to" the "power of the future" which, in its arrival in the kingdom of God, brings the fulfillment of the image even as Christ has proleptically revealed it. This corresponds to our earlier conclusion that man's being in the image is personal and historical being reflective of God's being as personal and historical. It follows that a subjective theory of value will not work either. Subjective value theory is based on autonomy. On the other hand, a strict objective theory of the good which abstracts the good from the structures of human experience in such a way as to depreciate in heteronomous fashion the autonomous functions of the self and history is also unsatisfactory.

In Christ, as the prolepsis of the kingdom of God, the principal obligation of the Christian ethic, love, is united with and given direction by the good, the fulfillment of man. Consequently, the Christian ethic of love will strive in its creative dynamic to run ahead toward the realization of what is given in promise. Indeed, as indicated in Thesis IV on the image, love draws both power and direction, indicative and imperative character, from the *imago Dei* as expressive of eschatological grace and promise and of eschatological good. Furthermore, this understanding of the matter corresponds to the previous observation that the image of God addresses us as both law and gospel: as law/imperative it judges while being simultaneously a guide to love for the person in Christ and as gospel it is the grace and power that initiates, motivates, and sustains love. The idea of the coinherence of the indicative and imperative is not a new one in Christian ethics. It acknowledges the "already–not yet" status of the Christian which the Reformers recognized in their observation that, while we are justified by grace through faith, the "old Adam" remains, locked in combat with the new man. Some have expressed this tension of the Christian life by describing its imperative as "Be what you are!" This seemingly paradoxical statement deserves to be retained but, recalling Moltmann's comment, we could well revise it slightly to underscore the essential futurity of man in the image of God: "Be what you will be!" The Christian life is the life of one who is *homo viator*.

A further implication of this futurist outlook on the good is that the Christian ethic should be an ethic of change not an ethic of "orders" as in the two kingdoms tradition and not an ethic of natural law as in the Scholastic tradition. These conceptions incorporate the dualisms we have explored and sought to resolve; they are built upon a static idea of God and history and they view the salvation of human fulfillment in the kingdom of God as beyond history rather than as its fulfillment and perfection. As Pannenberg has pointed out, if the end of the world is only ruin, then a static doctrine of "orders" to preserve a modicum of stability is very appropriate. However,

> . . . if the end of the world and its history, begun in Jesus, is seen also positively as its perfection in analogy with the resurrection of men, expected at this end, a resurrection in a world purified by divine judgment and transfigured by divine present, then Christian piety will be concerned with a change of everything present toward its perfection. For it is peculiar for the Christian faith that the end is no longer expected only as in the future, but becomes effective already as a power which determines the present and thus changes that which is present, just as this can be seen in the appearance of Jesus and his history and therefore is true of the Christian also.[20]

Consequently, Christian ethics needs to be an ethics of change. The idea of change in terms of repentance and renewal of life has always bulked large in Christian ethics as applied to the individual. Only recently has this notion of change been extended into the area of social structures. Even though we cannot hope to initiate the definitive society just as the individual, still plagued by the old Adam, cannot arrive at perfect Christlike humanity, Christians can surely initiate changes toward the realization of the universal values of the kingdom. Thus, Pannenberg submits that an ethics of change is appropriate for Christian ethics, one that ". . . conceives of man and his living conditions as a process. It sees him on the way from that which he is in actual fact to that which he can be and which he is according to his destiny."[21] An ethics built upon an eschatological theology of the kingdom of God is thoroughly historical and dynamic, a temporal model. Because the fulfillment of the *humanum* in the arrival of the kingdom is a future proleptically present to us in every present, continual transformation of the present is entailed in pursuit of the good. These comments lead directly into my final observation concerning the grounding of the good.

The eschatological nature of the *imago Dei,* which places it squarely within the context of the coming kingdom of God as the symbol of universal history, means that the distinction between personal and social ethics must be broken down. Such a distinction has normally reflected the sort of dualisms we have previously discussed. It has divided the Christian ethic between an ethic of law or natural law under the rubric of justice in the social order and an ethic of interpersonal and personal piety under the rubric of *agape* in the personal sphere. Such a division limits the scope of grace and implicitly restricts the redemptive significance of the kingdom of God to the salvation of individuals. The bifurcation of ethics in this fashion is a product of the dualism which divides man's nature and destiny according to historical and suprahistorical realities. The eschatological fulfillment of the *imago Dei,* as part and parcel of the universal kingdom of God, means that the full realization of the *humanum* participates in the sociopolitical, as well as personal, dimensions of the kingdom of God.[22] This makes the way into social ethics a clear path for Christian theology, one that proceeds from its vital center, a path that may be taken without special pleading.

Chapter IX

Deciding the Right

Having developed a particular vantage point on the theological foundations of the Christian ethic and having offered a theological and ontological grounding of the good, we need to suggest an apparatus for decision-making, a means by which we can decide the right in the situations of life. Such a normative theory of obligation should arise naturally out of the theological foundations. That is, constructive ethics should in its own realm give appropriate expression of the theological insights on which it is based.

It has been my impression in studying Christian ethics over a period of years that the correlation between theological foundations of ethics and the development of normative theory is frequently neglected. I do not wish to polemicize on this point but I do hold to the view that what makes the Christian ethic distinctive from other options in moral philosophy and religious ethics is the theological presuppositions which inform it. Those presuppositions should therefore have a determinative role in the process of selecting those forms of normative theory most appropriate to Christian decision-making. Paul Ramsey made an important contribution to the correlation of theological substance and ethical form in his book *Deeds and Rules in Christian Ethics.*[1] James Gustafson's well-known article "Context Versus Principles: A Misplaced Debate in Christian Ethics" has made a similar contribution.[2] Both have left contemporary Christian ethicists with the ongoing task of clarifying the relationship of theological foundations and normative theory. I have already begun that task in the previous chapter's discussion of the grounding of the good; I intend to continue it hereby indicating the extent to which the eschatological perspective of this work affects the development of normative theory.

THE QUESTION OF RULES

As we have seen, the grounding of the good in the eschatological doctrine of the image of God sets the values of human fulfillment, the values of the kingdom of God, before us as both law and gospel. The *agape* love revealed in Christ, who is the prolepsis of the kingdom and of true *imago* humanity, drives toward the fulfillment of these values. Indeed, as a mark of the eschatological humanity revealed in Christ, *agape* in motivation and action is itself an indication of humanization. The eschatological absoluteness of the kingdom values toward which love strives suggests that love is given specific definition by rules of obligation which concretize for us the sort of behavior that is creative of the good, the fulfillment of the *humanum*. In addressing the specific question of the nature of these rules, two things are evident from what has already been argued: (1) the rules of Christian ethics are person-oriented because they are derivative of the values that define the fulfillment of our humanity; (2) the rules of the Christian ethic should inculcate the law-gospel interplay that is implicit in the proleptic character of the kingdom of God and the human good. The question that needs answering, then, is precisely what concept of rules fulfills these criteria most adequately. We cannot hope to review the whole range of discussion on the matter of rules in ethics but we can at least look in an abstract way at two extremes before offering a third alternative.

The first general type of rule theory to consider would be some notion of prescriptive rules or prescriptive absolutes. Prescriptive rules legislate decision *a priori*. The classic example of this kind of rule is in traditional natural law morality. Right reason can discern the will of God within the structure of the created natural order. In this approach to ethics, rule determines decision. The moral agent is not involved in a struggle with the question of the right so much as he is faced with the task of discerning and understanding the applicable rule or rules. This approach inevitably leads to casuistry. Whatever consensus may exist concerning the primary rules of natural law morality, these rules must be extended through the deduction of further rules that will allow us to have a judgment on every conceivable circumstance of moral decision. Such an extension of rules will also include principles by which we may legislate behavior in connection with exceptions to the rules. Examples of casuistic exception-making rules are well known. For example, abortion is deemed contrary to natural law. Even in the instance where the mother's life is seriously threatened by carrying the baby to term, it is not a morally licit option. However, under the casuistic rule of "double effect," if a pregnant woman is diagnosed as having a uterine malignancy, for example, which threatens her life, the abortion that results from the surgery to remove the cancer is morally licit because the prime intention, namely, to save the woman's life, is in accord with natural law. The abortion here is not the intended effect but the secondary effect. This principle of double effect can be used in other circumstances to justify actions which appear contrary to natural law. One such instance would be when a physician decides to administer a pain-killer to a dying patient even though he knows it may well hasten the time of death. This effect is acceptable because it is the secondary effect of the primary and morally acceptable intention to relieve suffering.

The problem with prescriptive legalism and its attendant casuistry is not the existence of *a priori* rules *per se,* nor is it that casuistry does not represent a helpful and insightful form of moral reasoning. Indeed, casuistry is a form of acknowledging the situationally variant nature of many ethical decisions. The problem is rather the implicit presumption that we can know and do the right with absolute justification. This, it seems to me, is a method of moral justification that ignores the accusatory function of the law. The absence of this theological dimension in such a theory of rule-morality frustrates the law-gospel dynamic of the Christian life by tending toward works-righteousness and by obscuring the clear vision that we live the life of new obedience only by the power of the gospel.[3] The temptation here is for behavior to become oriented primarily to accurate conformity to rule and, thereby, self-justification rather than serious struggle to serve the needs of others. Beyond this, a theory of prescriptive absolutes, whether rooted in natural law or biblicistic authoritarianism, presumes a set pattern of moral knowledge that is inconsistent with the temporal ontology developed in this study. That is, it ignores or does not acknowledge the element of relativity in moral judgment that obtains in view of the proleptic character of the good and the "not yet" character of the kingdom of God.

If, by contrast to a theory of prescriptive rules, we were to operate with summary rules or rules as merely general guidelines we would also encounter problems.[4] A summary rule normally refers to a summary of the collective opinion of past ethical reflection on given moral questions. Summary rules function as guideposts to decision-making in the various situations of life. However, the question is left open as to the nature of the guidelines' claim on me as the moral agent. Are they merely advisory? If they are only guides and do not specifically prescribe are they not open to considerable subjective interpretation in any given situation? Certain advocates of situation ethics would be willing to treat the norms of Scripture and tradition as general guidelines or summary rules. According to the situationists, these general guidelines can help to illuminate the situation for us but they have no intrinsic claim on us—only love has that force—and they are subject to interpretation or even to being set aside when the situation demands something else of love than what the rule would appear to entail.

It is important to stress this point that the definition of rules as general guidelines or summary rules means that rules have no clear claim upon us. The result is that the dimension of law and gospel is threatened here too. A rule without genuine claim upon me can hardly carry the burden of the accusatory function of the law. If this is absent, the centrality of the gospel as the ground of the Christian life and ethic is also distorted. To live and love in the gospel is not to be free from the moral truth the law proclaims, nor is it to be free from its accusation; it is to be free from its coercion and condemnation. Accordingly, the confidence which the Christian brings to his ethical decision-making is this freedom and assurance of the gospel, *despite* his personal limitations in being able perfectly to know and do the right and to realize the good.

In situationism the emphasis is placed on the agent's capacity to interpret, with the assistance of summary rules, which action will bring the most loving consequence in a given circumstance. The guidance of general rules does not legislate behavior; it is the relative value of the possible ends that are likely to result from the alternatives presented that is ultimately determinative. Right and wrong are relative not only to the situation but also to the perception of the moral agent. Once more, the emphasis is on the ability of the agent to know and do the right in any circumstance. In this outlook the agent seeks to justify his decisions by demonstrating that the ends sought or achieved are the best possible in that situation. Beyond the command to love, there are no *a priori* rules as there are in legalism, but the dynamic is the same: moral decision and action are justified in virtue of their conformity to knowable criteria (rules for the legalist and ends for the situationist), and such justification is possible to determine in a given case because the agent possesses the capacity to know and do the right.[5] In situationism, as in legalism, the interplay of law and gospel is precluded as a formative element in ethical theory.

Summary rule theory, inasmuch as it is implicitly situational in the way I have described it, certainly allows for the measure of relativity that, as I suggested, is endemic to the human and world situation. However, it is a radical relativism that is more appropriate to the secularizing theologies we looked at in Chapter Three. By contrast, an ethic grounded in the conviction that the good is revealed and present to us in the prolepsis of the kingdom of God, while allowing for relativity in moral perception due to the eschatological character of the good, nonetheless recognizes the good as having been disclosed in its eschatological absoluteness and as making a continual impact on every present situation. This means that the norms which define love's drive toward the good are more than merely advisory in character.

The theological foundations of the Christian ethic that have been developed to this point lead me to believe that the rules of the Christian ethic should be neither prescriptive absolutes nor simply general guidelines. They are absolutes that lay claim on me as definitions of how love behaves in various situations of life. This makes them more than just guides; that is, they are not exposed to subjective reinterpretation or dismissal. They are, however, general as summary rules are general in not seeking to prescribe behavior in every situation of life through consistently literal enforcement or by casuistic extension.

These general absolutes of the Christian ethic which concretize *agape* and give expression to it I shall designate as *general rules.* The word "general" carries two meanings here: (1) it expresses their general or universal validity as absolutes which embody love's drive for the universal-eschatological values definitively; (2) it expresses their nonprescriptive character as an acknowledgment of the proleptic status of the good, which precludes legalism. Unlike the maxims of legalism, which are frequently understood to be obeyed for their own sake, these general rules derive their force and claim from their being subsumed under love's drive for the good. However, in that they do embody love, they participate in its absolute character and, therefore, accuse us in our failure even while they provide direction to a life whose sufficiency is in the gospel. Thus, these general rules of which I speak are not mere instruction and, yet, they are not pure judgment either.[6] *They also participate in the gospel promise. Inasmuch as these general rules concretely embody love's drive for the values of God's kingdom, they are statements of what God has promised to accomplish through his people by his grace and power.* This statement is a corollary of the understanding of eschatological theology that the present impact of the coming kingdom is the creative future of every present.

It is the further insight of the law-gospel dialectic in theology that the Christian, who is himself becoming (*homo viator*), pursues his ethic amid the ambiguities of a fallen world, a world that is in profound ways alienated from its own future in God. In this state of affairs there are several types of problems which commonly confront Christian decision-making. First of all, it is frequently difficult to discern the precise way in which a general rule should be applied in a given context of decision. The labyrinth of rationalization that sometimes occurs when one attempts a casuistic determination of rule-application in particularly complex situations graphically illustrates this problem. Secondly, we are all aware of the fact that conflicts between general rules often make certain decisions ambivalent. Thirdly, there is a continual challenge to probe the depths of past guidance for new formulations to express love's demands in the face of new and unprecedented problems such as those arising out of the advance of modern science and technology. Ours is a preliminary or penultimate situation in which God's kingdom has already been revealed and secured in the victory of Christ but not yet arrived and consummated in its eschatological perfection. For this reason, ambivalence and relativity will always be a part of moral decision in many instances. In view of this human and world situation, I must say that love's general rules are, according to their absolute character, immutable expressions of the claims which the good of the neighbor make upon us but they are so *prima facie*. In a fallen world our *prima facie* obligations may not always be our *actual* obligations in a given situation. General rules may not express the responsible choices actually open to us in every case.[7] In order to determine what our actual action or obligation ought to be in a given situation, the relevant *prima facie* general rule or rules must be brought into dialogue with that situation.

OUTLINE OF A DIALOGICAL ETHIC

The dialogue I refer to would include several areas of ethical reflection. In the first area of the dialogue there is a continual need for the church to translate general rule obligations into more precise statements having the character of "middle axioms," a notion made famous by John Bennett and originated by J. H. Oldham in his writings preparatory for the Oxford Conference of 1937. In the context of concern for Christian social ethics Bennett describes the "middle axiom" as "more concrete than a universal ethical principle and less specific than a program that includes legislation and political strategy."[8] Oldham's original definition of the concept which Bennett also quotes amplifies their nature further: "They are an attempt to define the directions in which, in a particular state of society, Christian faith must express itself. They are not binding for all time, but are provisional definitions of the type of behavior required of Christians at a given period and in given circumstances."[9] As an example of a "guiding principle"—we would say general rule—Bennett says in part, "We believe that the principle of cooperation and mutual concern, implicit in the moral order and essential to a just and durable peace, calls for a true community of nations. . . ."[10] Upon such a notion Bennett asserts there could hardly be disagreement.

The necessity of giving further definition to the concrete obligations that this principle implies requires then a middle axiom arising out of a dialogue with the situation. An example of such a middle axiom is offered by Bennett from the "Pillars of Peace" document produced in the wake of World War II by the old Federal Council of Churches' Commission on a Just and Durable Peace: "The peace must provide the political framework for a continuing collaboration of the United Nations and, in due course, of neutral and enemy nations."[11] More specific decision must still be made but the construction of the middle axiom which identifies the United Nations and the ultimate cooperation of neutral and enemy nations as the vehicle for the true community of nations, which the guiding principle requires, provides the sort of specificity required for decision.

Other areas of ethical reflection also lend themselves to the formulation of middle axioms as an adjunct to the decision. A prime example of this is in the area of the ethical concerns that have arisen due to rapid and unprecedented advances in medical technology. Scripture and tradition can supply us with general rules which deal with the preservation of human life and the relief of suffering, as well as insights on what constitutes the nature of truly "human" existence, but, in order to move from these general insights to decision in matters such as transplant surgery, genetic manipulation, and the euthanasia controversy, further interpretation is required. It is certainly the case that many or even all situations will have to be decided in terms of their individual characteristics but it is also necessary that in a field such as medicine there be some more specific guidelines brought to bear upon decision.[12]

It may well be that another field which could benefit from the effort to construct middle axioms would be the whole area of patterns of sexual behavior. The New Testament clearly offers us a high estimate of marriage and a considerable amount about what sexual union should exemplify, as well as prohibitions concerning certain forms of sexual abuse. However, further interpretation is needed if we are to have more specific guidance concerning the shifting patterns of marriage and premarital sex in modern society, the manner in which to approach homophile behavior in light of recent knowledge, and other problems resulting from advanced medical technology such as artificial insemination and transsexualism.

The second type of ethical reflection in the dialogue between general rules and situation is direct interpretation. It is frequently the case that the concrete actions which will represent most adequately the general rule obligations of love are not totally apparent in the situation. If we take as an example of a general rule the last portion of Luther's explanation to the fifth commandment as it appears in the *Small Catechism,* ". . . help and befriend him (our neighbor) in every necessity of life," we recognize that this general admonition requires specific decision in a variety of possible situations if it is to be implemented in our behavior. Such a general statement of obligation may be translated into middle axioms in select areas like social policy formation and medical procedure but probably not in day-to-day interpersonal relations. Here direct, intuitive decision is involved. Sometimes there is no difficulty in understanding the obligation; if I see a man in peril and distress I do not have much to debate about when it is within my power to respond in some way with help. However, when I confront my neighbor's needs in terms of his personal emotional and psychological formation the appropriate response is not so easy to discern. I am ultimately forced to take an interpretive risk in the process of decision.

Finally the third area of dialogue occurs when I find that two or more *prima facie* general rule obligations come into conflict with one another. Examples of such conflict in human experience are so commonplace that the point hardly needs illustration. Most frequently, we resolve the conflicts without extensive thought for they usually allow us little time for reflection and often represent a situation in which we feel that little is at stake. However, when we face such conflicts as that of the quality of life versus the preservation of life as in some cases of abortion and the care of the dying or obligations to honor parents versus obligations to wife and children, then the experience of conflict is intense. When decisional dialogue seeks to resolve conflicts it may find help consciously or subconsciously in the use of "adjudicating axioms."

George F. Thomas has called these "middle axioms." I have simply changed the terminology here to eliminate confusion with Oldham's and Bennett's use of the term, which we have just discussed and which is the more common sense of "middle axiom" in any case. Thomas lists the following axioms for the resolution of conflicting claims: (1) when, in the case of two competing claims upon my love, one determined to arise out of interest and the other out of need, the obligation to need takes precedence and the other claim is denied; (2) when we have conflicting obligations to two or more parties we may resolve this conflict by partially meeting the needs of all through the limitation or modification of our response. These first two axioms must be subjected to the two higher adjudicating principles of (3) "the gradation of higher and lower needs" which says that one may decide to favor one obligation over another on the grounds that one need is of a greater magnitude or character than the other; and (4) the principle of inclusiveness that directs us to that obligation which fulfills the needs of the greatest number of people possible.[13] These axioms contain no actual moral content in themselves; they simply guide reflection in cases of genuine or apparent conflict. They also do not prescribe adjudicating decision nor do they justify the compromise that is arrived at when one decides in accordance with such maxims. They do not eliminate the need for the risk of interpretive decision in the process of resolving compromise for they can be taken at face value simply to represent descriptions of how the mind might work in coping with conflict. As such they are useful for our system although they are certainly not peculiar to it.

In all the above aspects of the dialogue between general rules and the situations of ethical decision (the need to formulate middle axioms for the relative circumstances of history, the need for direct interpretation in the face of complex and uncertain situations, and the need for the resolution of conflicts by some form of compromise) there is an acknowledgment of the reality of an inescapable dimension of relativity and penultimacy which the proleptic structure of existence comprehends as an ontological fact and which the theology of sin and grace in the eschatological perspective on the doctrine of the image recognizes as a theological necessity. Practically speaking this also means that there is in the dialogical interplay of general rules and situation an irreducible element of intuition involved in decision-making. This makes it clear that there is also an abiding element of risk in ethical decision. Therefore, it is important to realize that the sufficiency of the Christian is always in the gospel. This comes clearly into view when we examine the interplay of law and gospel that occurs throughout the dialogical process. The traditional understanding of this interplay is not obviated by our eschatological orientation. Indeed, as we observed in the formulation of our third thesis on the image of God in man the law-gospel dialectic is implicit in this proleptic structure of human existence.

To put this, then, in terms of the Christian's experience of the process of the dialogical ethic I have just outlined, we would begin by saying that the Christian experiences first the accusation of the law that uncovers his need for the gospel. The experience of God's forgiveness and promise in the gospel ushers the Christian into a new life of faith and trust. It is the freedom to love as he has been loved, which God's grace accomplishes, that sets in motion the Christian life under the imperative "Be what you will be!" Love's drive toward the good is informed then, as I have said, by general rule obligations—rules that express what the Christian *can* do by grace. When these come into dialogue with the situations of life and culminate in decision, the ambivalence of sinful existence and the relativity of the "not yet," penultimate, character of our historical circumstance make it apparent that in the translation of *prima facie* general rule obligations into decisions determining our *actual* obligations there results an ineluctable element of compromise and uncertainty which indicates that our realization of the good can only be fragmentary at best. In the midst of this realization the Christian experiences the judgment of the law through its general rule representatives. He is therefore returned to the gospel, recognizing that herein lies his only justification and, ultimately, the only ultimate justification of his moral judgments, notwithstanding their theoretical justification.

This phenomenon is unlike either the teleologist, who feels his moral judgments to be justified by a calculus of the good produced, or the deontologist who feels his judgments to be justified by their conformity to the known right. Both run the risk of legalism which presumes that men can somehow attain to the good and the right. The justification of our actions is easily elided into the justification of ourselves. This is perhaps most apparent when legalism employs casuistic extension of basic principles to demonstrate how our actions in exception to these basic principles are in reality in conformity with them in virtue of their conformity to principles which legitimate the exceptions.

Finally, the dialogue between general rule obligations and the relative situations of life is also expressive of the interplay of the absolute and the relative. The expressions of the absolute in our *prima facie* general rules are subject to being modified in certain situations through relative middle axioms which interpret their meaning contextually, and by some form of choice or compromise in the resolution of conflict. However, the *prima facie* rules as representative of the absolute in terms of the transcendent future values of the kingdom also bring the force of judgment and grace upon the situation. They do not simply suffer the modification of circumstance but represent in "inprincipled" form the transforming impact of the future kingdom of God on the "not yet" character of the present. This is their proleptic nature, and, indeed, the entire dialogical interchange between general rule and situation, as a dialogue between absolute and relative, exhibits the proleptic structure of the good, man's fulfillment proleptically present in his being as *imago Dei*— a good which the rules project and the dialogue seeks to attain.

Certainly the list of general rules needs investigation and clarification, and it may well be that no consensus is possible on what should be included on the list. From this author's viewpoint one certainly ought to begin with the Decalogue, our Lord's commentary on the moral law in the Sermon on the Mount, the apostolic imperatives, and time-honored catechetical commentary on the moral law in the history of Christian thought. Certainly, in both Scripture and tradition, there will be a need to draw distinctions between what is truly general rule expression of the values of the transcendent future and what is in the nature of a middle axiom spoken to the relativities of an historical present at some point in history. This is the ongoing task of the ethicist in tandem with the exegete. It lies beyond the scope of our work here.

DEONTOLOGY OR TELEOLOGY?

The Christian ethic as envisioned here can be neither a deontology nor a teleology strictly speaking but one that unites aspects of both. In a deontological theory we recall that the obligations are understood as given *a priori* to be embraced for their own sake. There is no theoretical consideration of ends in the justification of moral judgments. This betrays the sort of ahistorical and transcendental mentality typical of much of the dualism inherent in the tradition of theological reflection on the *imago Dei*. It is subject to the sorts of criticism we have seen Tillich level against heteronomy.

Teleology regards the right as determined by the ends achieved. Such an approach thrives best in a view of man's nature and destiny that is historical and developmental. While this avoids the dualism of the transcendental mentality, it does so at the cost of ignoring the inescapable dualism between what we are and what we will be by grace, a dualism which is the consequence of sin. For this very reason, I was critical, in Chapter Three, of Schleiermacher's evolutionary view of man in the image of God. On the same grounds I have been critical throughout this thesis of all progressivist views of the image of God and of eschatology. The general presuppositions of teleology are subject to the sorts of criticism we have seen Tillich level against autonomy. The fact that the universal kingdom of God as an historical-eschatological concept brings together in continuity the this-worldly and other-worldly aspects of man's nature and destiny under the rubric of the historical-eschatological concept of the image of God as an expression of the good means that neither the transcendental, heteronomous bent of deontology nor the historical, autonomous bent of teleology will in themselves suffice for our ethic.

To the extent that we have made the good our starting point and the attainment of the good our focus, the ethic is teleological in character. It is also the case that the eschatological vision with which we have been working indicates the continual possibility of the arrival of the genuinely "new" as preliminary, but significant realizations of the good within the contingencies of history. Certainly it should be the faith and expectation of the Christian life that these proleptic moments continue to occur throughout history. History possesses openness and possibility in the face of the coming kingdom as its fulfillment. In this regard too there is a teleological character to eschatological ethics.

On the other hand, there is also a decidedly deontological orientation in our ethic as well. The values of the kingdom of God which we find focused in human fulfillment are proleptically present to us in the Christ as *the* image of God. As such they are present to us *a priori* in accordance with the ontological priority of the future in which they participate. The general rules which define the right, love's obligation to the good, are therefore also given as *a priori*. This is clearly a feature of deontology as one can observe in the case of Kant who also defines the right as *a priori*. Moreover, this leads into another feature of the Christian ethic which also brings it close to deontology.

Kant states that the only true good is the good will. This illustrates his concern and all deontological concern for agent morality, for the importance of motive in the justification of moral judgments. Kant's categorical imperative is in essence a formal way to encapsulate what is required if the good will would respond to the *a priori* right for its own sake without eudaemonistic motive. The categorical imperative therefore stands over against the agent in much the same position as that of a divine lawgiver. Now we have said that the proleptic revelation of the image of God in Christ stands over against man as law and gospel. It judges man in terms of his alienation from his own being, and yet, nonetheless, it promises his fulfillment of that being by grace. In ethical terms, inasmuch as this image is also a locus of the good, it guides man's moral efforts and it judges man's failure to attain that good. But, most importantly, because that good is bestowed on man by grace through faith in Christ, it also enables man to love and to seek for others the good that he has himself been given. That is, the Christian ethic is an ethic of freedom from eudaemonistic motive, even as Luther understood this in the *Treatise on Christian Liberty*.

Fear for one's destiny is a bondage of the past which is obliterated by the gift of the future. This traditional, biblical understanding of Christian ethics as an ethic of freedom is underscored also by the previous observation under the first thesis on the *imago Dei* that futurity is the concomitant of freedom and that God as power of the future is the source of human freedom in view of man's participation in that future as God's image. The net effect of these thoughts is that love as *the* principle of obligation in the Christian ethic is the counterpart of Kant's "good will" because it proceeds toward the good purely for its own sake in view of its eschatological freedom from concern for self. The difference, of course, is that the freedom that enables the motive of *agape* is grounded outside man and comes to him as a gift. This fundamental insight of the Christian faith is expressed perhaps most prominently in justification *sola gratia* but it is also contained in our earlier conclusions that man in the *image of God* is so, derivatively, dependently, theomorphically. If one were forced to decide as to whether our perspective on the Christian ethic more closely resembled teleology or deontology, the profound nature of these characteristics shared with deontology would perhaps ultimately favor the latter.

A THEONOMOUS ETHIC

The ethic of the kingdom under the rubric of the doctrine of the image of God in man will be neither a heteronomous nor an autonomous ethic. Each response to the norms of the kingdom will be a fragmentary prolepsis of the fulfillment of humanity, of the promised future union of men with God and men with men in union with God, a promised future which is constitutive of our being as men in the present. Thus, the goal of love will not be obedience to transcendent norms from outside history which calls upon us to overcome and negate history within history (heteronomy) nor will it be an ethic guided by the conviction that man is capable of the good within history and the source of his own law (autonomy). Rather, love's desire will be to realize by its action—albeit in a fragmentary way— a witness in history that is transparent to the ultimate synthesis with the transcendent promised in the fulfillment of history. Here as in the eschatological image from which we have taken our point of departure there is no bifurcation of man's understanding of the good. The pessimism of transcendental heteronomy concerning historical existence, which leads to a dualistic ethic of two realms or a division between nature and grace, is overcome by the realization that the good as the fulfillment of the *humanum* is understood in terms of a doctrine of the *imago Dei* which states the continuity of historical existence and existence in God: "The image of God refers to the distinctive way in which man's whole being as personal and historical being reflects God's being as personal and historical being" (Thesis I). At the same time, the undue optimism of autonomy is prevented by the additional insight that the good present is only proleptically present. Moreover, the kingdom which brings in the fulfillment of the good is God's kingdom and not the product of human striving and developmental process. This fact has been undergirded by the repeated observation that the eschatological promise of the image of God, in its being a *promise,* bears witness to the reality that man as *image* of God is *only* image.

It follows from all that has been presented to this point that the Christian ethic finds its place in the witnessing function of the church. For the church, as the Body of Christ, is through its witness to the Christ, the continuance in history of his proleptic revelation of the kingdom of God. As such, the proclamation of the church, the life-style of the church, the communion of the church, and its creative action in personal and sociopolitical relations, all constitute concretions of the prolepsis—albeit in a fragmentary way—which the church is called to be. As Ernst Käsemann has written concerning St. Paul's theology, "Through thick and thin, Paul holds to the view that God activates his righteousness not in a renewed, but in a totally new covenant, and the apostle can thus legitimately transfer the motif of the people of God on to the Christians as the eschatological Israel."[14] This new covenant is a covenant of faith and hope in which the eschatological salvation includes the need and promise for man to become human. To this end, it is through the faithful, as agents of his kingdom, that God chooses to manifest his righteousness on earth.

Notes and Index

Notes

Chapter I.
The Search for Man: An Introduction

1. Jürgen Moltmann has written *Mensch: Christliche Anthropologie in den Konflickten der Gegenwart* (Stuttgart: Kreuz-Verlag, 1971), and Wolfhart Pannenberg has more pointedly brought the eschatological perspective to bear on Christian anthropology in his book *What Is Man?* trans. Duane Priebe (Philadelphia: Fortress, 1970). In ethics the principal effort in behalf of eschatological theology would be several essays in Carl E. Braaten's *Eschatology and Ethics* (Minneapolis: Augsburg, 1974).
2. H. Richard Niebuhr, *Christ and Culture*, Harper Torchbooks (New York: Harper & Row, 1956).
3. Luther's principal statement on the two kingdoms occurs in "Temporal Authority: To What Extent It Should Be Obeyed," *The Christian in Society*, vol. 45 of *Luther's Works*, ed. Helmut T. Lehmann and Walther I. Brandt (Philadelphia: Fortress, 1962). See also Heinrich Bornkamm, *Luther's Doctrine of the Two Kingdoms*, Facet Books Social Ethics Series, 14, trans. Karl H. Hertz (Philadelphia: Fortress, 1966).
4. Brian F. Skinner, *Beyond Freedom and Dignity* (New York: Knopf, 1971).
5. Dean E. Wooldridge, *Mechanical Man* (New York: McGraw-Hill, 1968), pp. 189ff.
6. James B. Nelson, *Human Medicine* (Minneapolis: Augsburg, 1973), p. 26.
7. Ibid., p. 18.
8. Paul Ramsey, *The Patient as Person* (New Haven & London: Yale University Press, 1970), p. xi.
9. Harmon Smith, *Ethics and the New Medicine* (Nashville: Abingdon, 1970), *passim*.
10. Ian Barbour, *Science and Secularity* (New York & London: Harper & Row, 1970), p. 93.
11. Leon Kass, "The New Biology: What Price Relieving Man's Estate?" in *Readings on Ethical and Social Issues in Biomedicine*, ed. Richard W. Wertz (Englewood Cliffs, N.J.: Prentice-Hall, 1973), pp. 66–69. Originally in *Science* 174 (November 19, 1971), pp. 779–88.
12. Leroy Augenstein, *Come Let Us Play God* (New York & London: Harper & Row, 1969), p. 141.

13. Paul Tillich, "The Person in a Technical Society," in *Varieties of Modern Social Theory*, ed. Hendrick Ruitenbeck (New York: E. P. Dutton, 1963), pp. 287–303.

14. Roger Shinn, *Man: The New Humanism, New Directions in Theology Today*, 6 (Philadelphia: Westminster, 1968), pp. 62–70.

15. Victor Ferkiss, *Technological Man: The Myth and the Reality* (New York: George Braziller, 1969), p. 246.

16. Ibid., pp. 250–55.

17. Ibid., p. 256.

18. Emil Brunner, *Man in Revolt: A Christian Anthropology*, trans. Olive Wyon (Philadelphia: Westminster, 1947), p. 92.

Chapter II.
Dichotomized Man

1. Carl E. Braaten, *The Future of God* (New York & London: Harper & Row, 1969), pp. 44–45. Jean Danielou also makes the point that the church's condemnation of Origen's *apocatastasis* theology was essentially a condemnation of its resemblance to the Platonic theory of *metempsychosis* and not a repudiation of the idea of salvation as a restoration to lost origins. *Origen*, trans. Walter Mitchell (New York: Sheed and Ward, 1955), p. 289.

2. Gustaf Wingren, *Man and the Incarnation*, trans. Ross Mackenzie (Philadelphia: Fortress, 1959), p. ix.

3. Emil Brunner, *Man in Revolt: A Christian Anthropology*, trans. Olive Wyon (Philadelphia: Westminster, 1947), pp. 503–4; David Cairns, *The Image of God in Man* (New York: Philosophical Library, 1953), pp. 74–75.

4. Irenaeus, *Against Heresies*, V, 6, 1.

5. Cairns, *The Image of God*, pp. 75–77.

6. Ibid., p. 78, citing Lawson, *Biblical Theology of St. Irenaeus*.

7. Irenaeus, *Against Heresies*, V, 16, 2.

8. Brunner, *Man in Revolt*, p. 93.

9. Irenaeus, *Against Heresies*, III, 18, 1. Here Irenaeus seems to be saying, contrary to our previous analysis, that both the image and likeness are lost in the fall. However, the bulk of the passages support the conclusion that the image remains while the likeness is lost. Cairns's suggestion that this is probably just an instance of careless inconsistency seems reasonable. *The Image of God*, p. 75.

10. Irenaeus, *Against Heresies*, III, 18, 7.

11. The circular pattern of restoration eschatology seems apparent when the Greek Fathers speak of "divinization" as their key term for understanding the process of salvation which God's grace initiates. Divinization is quite clearly thought of as a restoration to the pure state of Adam's original condition. See Nicholas Gloubokowsky, "Grace in the Greek Orthodox Fathers (to St. John of Damascus) and Inter-Church Union," *The Doctrine of Grace*, ed. W. T. Whitely (New York: Macmillan, 1931), pp. 72–73.

12. The principal sources for Clement's doctrine of the image are: *The Exhortation to the Heathen*, *Stromata*, and *The Instructor*.

13. Both Emil Brunner and Helmut Thielicke agree in linking the development of Aquinas's thinking on the image to the distinction between image and likeness initiated by Irenaeus. However, it should be noted that Thomas himself does not repeat the same exegesis of Gen. 1:26 that we have witnessed in Irenaeus and Clement. Rather, as evidenced in *Summa Theologia*, part I, question 93, art. 9, Thomas sees the "likeness" as something more general than the "image" and included in the idea of the image. Therefore, the influence of Irenaeus must be understood not in terms of his exegesis but in terms of the distinction which the exegesis produced. This is how Thielicke puts the matter. See Brunner, *Man in Revolt*, pp. 506–7, and Helmut Thielicke, *Theological Ethics*, vol. 1, ed. William Lazareth (Philadelphia: Fortress, 1966), pp. 202–3.

14. Aquinas, *Summa Theologia*, part I, question 93, arts. 3, 4, 6, 8.

15. Ibid., part I, question 93, art. 5 (italics in original text).

16. Ibid., art. 8.

17. Ibid., question 95, art. 1.

18. Ibid., part III, question 109, art. 2.

19. Thielicke, *Theological Ethics*, pp. 210–11.

20. Ibid., p. 211.

21. Paul Tillich, *Systematic Theology*, vol. 3 (Chicago: The University of Chicago Press, 1963), pp. 12–15. As a corollary of this in the realm of epistemology, Tillich has referred to the Thomistic system as representing a *dissolution* of the Augustinian solution. That is, by contrast to Augustine's ontological approach to the knowledge of God, Tillich believes that Thomas creates a radical discontinuity between the knowledge available to reason and that which is available to faith. Analogous to the distinction between nature and grace, which we have been dealing with here is Tillich's observation that since for Aquinas reason's knowledge of God and the good is purely mediate, faith's knowledge is superior and finally becomes faith in authority, the blind acceptance of supernatural knowledge. "Two Types of Philosophy of Religion," *Theology of Culture*, ed. Robert C. Kimball (New York: Oxford University Press, 1959), pp. 16ff.

22. Paul Tillich, "Christentum und Socialismus (I)," *Gessamlte Werke*, 2 (Stuttgart: Evangelisches Verlagswerk, 1962), p. 25.

23. H. Richard Niebuhr, *Christ and Culture*, Harper Torchbooks (New York: Harper & Row, 1956), p. 146. It is in sensitivity to this dualism of which we speak that Karl Rahner has called for an expansion of the scope of grace. Rahner points out that the standard post-Tridentine view of nature and grace, which he feels was probably read back into the Scholastics where it did not actually exist, has compartmentalized nature and grace so that grace is a superstructure that does not make its presence felt in the realm of self-contained nature where man experiences himself and is presented to himself. In contrast to this grace-nature dichotomy, modern thought demands a comprehensive, integrated synthetic view of the "whole" man such that man can experience the reality of grace in the realm of nature where he experiences himself. Grace is far more compre-

hensive in scope than it is when understood in terms of quantities of created grace dispensed sacramentally by the church. Rather grace permeates all of reality.

In addition, Rahner also sees the law-gospel correlation of Lutheran theology as contributing to the same dichotomy between nature and grace. To the extent to which it has contributed to the two kingdoms view in which a static world under the sway of the orders of creation is allowed to exist in paradoxical coexistence with a kingdom under the sway of the gospel, this Lutheran tradition has also contributed to the bifurcation of human existence. Karl Rahner, *Nature and Grace* (London: Sheed and Ward, 1963), pp. 5–44.

24. Martin Luther, *Lectures on Genesis*, vol. 1 of *Luther's Works*, trans. George V. Schick, ed. Jaroslav Pelikan (St. Louis: Concordia Publishing House, 1958–), pp. 60ff.

25. Ibid., p. 60.

26. Ibid., pp. 62–63.

27. Ibid., p. 65.

28. Brunner, *Man in Revolt*, p. 94.

29. Ibid., p. 508.

30. Luther, *Lectures on Genesis*, p. 61.

31. Cairns, *The Image of God*, pp. 122–26.

32. Luther, *Lectures on Genesis*, p. 67.

33. Francis Pieper, *Christian Dogmatics*, vol. 1, trans. Theodore Engelder et al. (St. Louis: Concordia Publishing House, 1950), pp. 518–19. This distinction between the "wider" and the "proper" sense of the image is also spoken of by the dogmaticians in terms of the image as understood *generically* and *figuratively* or *specifically* and *literally*. Heinrich Schmid, *The Doctrinal Theology of the Evangelical Lutheran Church*, 3d ed., revised, trans. from the German and Latin by Charles A. Hay and Henry E. Jacobs (Minneapolis: Augsburg, 1961), p. 223.

34. *The Book of Concord*, trans. and ed. Theodore G. Tappert (Philadelphia: Fortress, 1959), *Apology to the Augsburg Confession*, IV, 24; XVIII, 9; see also Brunner, *Man in Revolt*, p. 508.

35. Kjell Ove Nilsson, *Simul, Das Miteinander von Göttlichem und Menschlichem in Luthers Theologie* (Göttingen: Vandenhoek & Ruprecht, 1966), pp. 83–87.

36. Ibid., pp. 86–87.

37. Luther, *Lectures on Genesis*, pp. 56–57.

38. See Braaten, *The Future of God*, pp. 145–52.

39. Tillich, *Systematic Theology*, vol. 3, pp. 355–56.

Chapter III.
Secularized Man

1. Roger Shinn, *Man: The New Humanism, New Directions in Theology Today*, 6 (Philadelphia: Westminster, 1968), p. 50.

2. Ibid.

3. Ibid., p. 51.

4. Richard R. Niebuhr, *Schleiermacher on Christ and Religion* (New York: Charles Scribner's Sons, 1964), pp. 182ff. gives us a helpful summary explanation of Schleiermacher's characterization of religion as a feeling of absolute dependence (God-consciousness): "Piety or religion is the name of the level of self-consciousness that is most decisive of all . . . when personal existence and destiny are our chief concern. This level of consciousness has for its content the irreducible givenness of the self. . . . This consciousness, moreover, involves a feeling sense of dependence or a sense of having been posited in-such-and-such-a-way. . . . Consequently, the religiousness that is native to man, constitutive of his nature, and the fundamental problematic of his existence is not to be confused with any supposed intuition of, or immediacy with, the Absolute. That which is immediate to the self is simply and solely the self as dependent."

5. Friedrich Schleiermacher, *The Christian Faith*, English translation of the second German edition, ed. H. R. Mackintosh and J. S. Stewart (Philadelphia: Fortress, 1976), paragraph 59.

6. Ibid., paragraph 61.

7. Ibid.

8. Ibid., paragraph 60.

9. Ibid., paragraph 61.

10. Ibid., paragraphs 70–73.

11. Niebuhr, *Schleiermacher*, pp. 214–28.

12. Richard B. Brandt makes the point that for Schleiermacher religion (the function of the God-consciousness) is a unique activity of the human spirit which is an autonomous activity grounded in the universal essence of mankind. It is the original property of the human mind. *The Philosophy of Schleiermacher* (New York: Greenwood Press, 1968), p. 305.

13. H. Richard Niebuhr, *The Meaning of Revelation* (New York: Macmillan, 1960), p. 20. See also note 4 above.

14. Schleiermacher, *The Christian Faith*, paragraph 60; pp. 157–69. Emil Brunner observed that "Schleiermacher, (as usual) under the cloak of a re-formulation of the Christian doctrine, actually gives up the fundamental Christian view of the origin of man, and substitutes for it an idealistic, evolutionary theory with a strongly naturalistic bent; for the idea of the origin in Creation he substitutes that of the goal of evolution of a universal spiritual process." *Man in Revolt: A Christian Anthropology*, trans. Olive Wyon (Philadelphia: Westminster, 1947), p. 87.

15. Schleiermacher, *The Christian Faith*, paragraph 169.

16. "Justification and Reconciliation," chap. VI, quoted in Niebuhr, *Christ and Culture*, Harper Torchbooks (New York: Harper & Row, 1956), p. 98.

17. Ibid., p. 99.

18. Norman Metzler, "The Ethics of the Kingdom" (Ph.D. dissertation, University of Munich, 1971), p. 202.

19. Ibid.

20. Ibid., pp. 221ff.

21. Ibid., p. 382.

22. E. L. Mascall, *The Secularization of Christianity* (New York: Holt, Rinehart & Winston, 1965), pp. 213–14.

23. Paul M. van Buren, *The Secular Meaning of the Gospel* (New York and London: Macmillan & Collier-Macmillan Ltd., 1966), p. xiv.

24. Ibid., pp. 19–20.

25. Ibid., pp. 97–99.

26. Ibid., pp. 104–5.

27. Ibid., p. 99.

28. Ibid., p. 103.

29. Ibid., p. 105.

30. Ibid., p. 103.

31. Ibid., p. 102.

32. Ibid., pp. 197–98.

33. Ibid., pp. 126–34.

34. Ibid., p. 163.

35. Ibid., p. 154.

36. For a fine example of this, see the thorough critical analysis of Mascall, *The Secularization of Christianity*, pp. 40–105.

37. Carl Braaten and Robert Jenson, *The Futurist Option* (New York & Toronto: Newman, 1970), pp. 31–32.

38. Ibid., p. 45.

39. Ibid., pp. 31–58 *passim.*

40. Harvey Cox, *The Secular City*, revised edition (New York: Macmillan, 1966), pp. 211–12.

41. Ibid., pp. 213–35.

42. Ibid., pp. 19–21.

43. Ibid., pp. 95–98.

44. Ibid., p. 114.

45. Ibid., p. 97.

46. Shinn, *Man*, p. 146.

47. Rudolf Bultmann, "New Testament and Mythology," *Kerygma and Myth*, ed. Hans Werner Bartsch, trans. Reginald Fuller (New York: Harper & Row, 1961), pp. 3–4.

48. Ibid., p. 5.

49. Ibid., p. 24. Rudolf Bultmann, *Jesus Christ and Mythology* (New York: Charles Scribner's Sons, 1958), pp. 53ff.

50. Bultmann, *Jesus Christ and Mythology*, pp. 11–18.

51. Ibid., p. 31.

52. Bultmann, *Kerygma and Myth*, p. 32.

53. Martin Heidegger, *Being and Time*, trans. John Macquarrie and Edward Robinson (New York: Harper & Row, 1962), pp. 445–47. Rudolf Bultmann, *Existence and Faith*, trans. Schubert M. Ogden (Cleveland: World, 1960), pp. 102ff.

54. "Jesus Christ is the eschatological event not as an established fact of past time but as repeatedly present, as addressing you and me here and now in preaching." Rudolf Bultmann, *History and Eschatology: The Presence of Eternity* (New York: Harper & Row, 1957), p. 152.

55. Ibid., p. 155.

56. Rudolf Bultmann, *Theology of the New Testament*, vol. 1, trans. Kendrick Grobel (New York: Charles Scribner's Sons, 1951), pp. 19–20.

Chapter IV.
Theonomous Man

1. Augustine, *The Trinity*, XV, 1.
2. Ibid., XII, 7. See also in *Joan Evang.*, XXIII, 10: "There is a truth in man which is the imaged reflection of the truth in God. For not in the body but in the mind was man made in the image of God. In his own likeness (*similitudine*) let us seek God, in his own image recognize the Creator." Quoted in Roger Hazelton, "The Devotional Life," *A Companion to the Study of St. Augustine*, ed. Roy W. Battenhouse (New York: Oxford University Press, 1956), p. 405.
3. Augustine, *The Trinity*, XIV, 6.
4. Reinhold Niebuhr, *The Nature and Destiny of Man*, vol. 1, (New York: Charles Scribner's Sons, 1964), pp. 154–58. Niebuhr also cites the *Confessions* as indicating that for Augustine the power of transcendence places him so outside everything else that he can find a home only in God: "I dive on this side and on that, as far as I can and there is no end. So great is the force of memory, so great is the force of life, even in the mortal life of man. What shall I do then, O Thou my true life my God? I will pass beyond this power of mine which is called memory; yea, I will pass beyond it that I may approach unto Thee. O sweet Light . . . And where shall I find Thee? If I find thee without my memory then I do not retain Thee in my memory. And how shall I find Thee if I remember Thee not?" X, 7–17.
5. Paul Tillich, *A History of Christian Thought*, ed. Carl E. Braaten (New York: Harper & Row, 1968), pp. 108–9.
6. Emil Brunner, *Man in Revolt: A Christian Anthropology*, trans. Olive Wyon (Philadelphia: Westminster, 1947), p. 406. See Augustine, *The Trinity*, XIII, XIV, 2.
7. *Joan. Evang.* XXIII, 10, quoted in Hazelton, "The Devotional Life," p. 405.
8. Ibid., p. 406.
9. *Enarrations on the Psalms*, 118, quoted in Hazelton, "The Devotional Life," p. 406.
10. Ibid., p. 158.
11. Cyril Richardson, "The Enigma of the Trinity," *A Companion to the Study of St. Augustine*, ed. Roy W. Battenhouse (New York: Oxford University Press, 1956), pp. 248–49. See in *The Trinity*, VII, 6; IX, 2; XII, 6; XV, 1, 20; X, 12. In *The Spirit and the Letter*, 48 (xxviii) Augustine makes a positive statement concerning the abiding existence of the image of God in man but the negative aspects are also clear and relevant at this point: "Yet we must remember that the image of God in the human soul has not been so completely obliterated by the stain of earthly affections, that no faint outlines of the original remain therein."
12. Paul Tillich, *Theology of Culture*, ed. Robert C. Kimball (New York: Oxford University Press, 1959), pp. 12–13.
13. Ibid., pp. 13–16.
14. Ibid., pp. 16–19.
15. Augustine, *Enchiridion*, XXVI, XXVII; *The City of God*, XIII, xiv–

xxiii. In these chapters Augustine also takes pains to distinguish himself from the Platonists with regard to the soul-body dichotomy, the possibility of earthly bodies being made incorruptible and eternal, and the fact that the spiritual body of the resurrection is indeed spiritual.

16. Augustine, *Enchiridion*, LXXXIX–XCII.

17. Augustine, *The City of God*, XIII, 19–23. On the perfections of the end when all things will be made new see, e.g., XIX, 11–12; XXI, 15.

18. Ibid., XXII, 16; esp. *The Trinity*, XIV, 16; XV, 8.

19. Brunner, *Man*, pp. 84–96.

20. Ernst Benz, *Evolution and Christian Hope*, trans. Heinz G. Frank (Garden City, N.Y.: Doubleday, 1966), pp. 25–34.

21. Carl E. Braaten, *The Future of God* (New York & London: Harper & Row, 1969), p. 146.

22. Heinrich Bornkamm, *Luther's Doctrine of the Two Kingdoms*, trans. Karl H. Hertz, Facet Books Social Ethics Series, 14 (Philadelphia: Fortress, 1966), pp. 19–28.

23. Tillich, *A History of Christian Thought*, p. 112.

24. Ibid., p. 105.

25. Ibid., p. 117.

26. See, for example, Paul Tillich, *Systematic Theology*, vol. 1 (Chicago: The University of Chicago Press, 1951), pp. 64–65.

27. Ibid., pp. 258–59.

28. Ibid., p. 259.

29. Tillich, *Systematic Theology*, vol. 2, pp. 32–33; "Symbolically speaking, it is the image of God in man which gives the possibility of the Fall. Only he who is the image of God has the power of separating himself from God. His greatness and his weakness are identical. Even God could not remove the one without removing the other. And if man had not received this possibility, he would have been a thing among things, unable to serve the divine glory, either in salvation or in condemnation. Therefore, the doctrine of the Fall has always been treated as the doctrine of the Fall of man, although it was also seen as a cosmic event."

30. Ibid., p. 49.

31. Ibid.

32. Paul Tillich, *Dynamics of Faith*, Harper Torchbooks (New York: Harper and Brothers, 1958), pp. 4–9.

33. Ibid., p. 9.

34. Paul Tillich, "Church and Culture," *Interpretation of History* (New York & London: Charles Scribner's Sons, 1936), p. 234.

35. Paul Tillich, "Religion and Secular Culture," *The Protestant Era*, abridged edition, trans. James Luther Adams (Chicago: The University of Chicago Press, 1957), pp. 56–57.

36. Ibid.

37. Tillich, "Christentum und Socialismus (I)," p. 25.

38. Tillich, *Interpretation of History*, p. 278.

39. Tillich, "Historical and Non-Historical Interpretations of History," *Protestant Era*, p. 27.

40. See Carl Braaten's article which analyzes the tension between Tillich's historical-eschatological side and his ahistorical ontological side (Tillich I and Tillich II). Dr. Braaten concludes that ontology triumphs over his-

tory. "Eschatology and Ontology in Conflict: A study of Paul Tillich's Theology," *Christ and Counter-Christ* (Philadelphia: Fortress, 1972), pp. 54–66.

41. Tillich, *Systematic Theology*, vol. 3, p. 407.

42. Tillich feels that he has avoided Greek dualism in that the concept of essentialization includes the whole being of man. So in speaking of the resurrection he states: "Resurrection says mainly that the Kingdom of God includes all dimensions of being. The whole personality participates in Eternal Life. If we use the term "essentialization," we can say that man's psychological spiritual and social being is implied in his bodily being— and this in unity with the essences of everything else that has being." Ibid., p. 413.

43. Ibid., pp. 415, 420.

Chapter V.
The Recovery of Eschatology

1. Klaus Koch, *The Rediscovery of Apocalyptic*, Studies in Biblical Theology, second series 22, trans. Margaret Kohl (London: SCM, 1972), pp. 36ff.

2. Paul D. Hanson, *The Dawn of Apocalyptic* (Philadelphia: Fortress, 1975), pp. 4–6. See also Hanson's articles "Jewish Apocalyptic Against Its Near Eastern Environment," *Revue Biblique* 78 (January 1971), pp. 31–58 and "Old Testament Apocalyptic Reexamined," *Interpretation* 25, 4 (October 1971), pp. 454–79.

3. See Koch's review of von Rad's development on the subject of apocalyptic, *The Rediscovery of Apocalyptic*, pp. 42–47. Koch credits von Rad with laying out the subject of apocalyptic as an historical problem before the general theological audience.

4. Hanson, *The Dawn of Apocalyptic*, pp. 7–12.

5. Ernst Käsemann, "The Beginnings of Christian Theology," *New Testament Questions of Today*, trans. W. J. Montague (Philadelphia: Fortress, 1969), p. 102.

6. Ibid., pp. 96–97.

7. Carl E. Braaten, "Apocalyptic Interpretation of History," *Christ and Counter-Christ* (Philadelphia: Fortress, 1972), pp. 5–7. Consult Ulrich Wilckens, "The Understanding of Revelation within the History of Primitive Christianity," *Revelation as History*, ed. Wolfhart Pannenberg, trans. David Granskou (New York: Macmillan, 1968), pp. 57–121.

8. Braaten, "Apocalyptic Interpretation of History," p. 7.

9. Wolfhart Pannenberg, "The Crisis of the Scripture Principle," *Basic Questions in Theology*, vol. 1, trans. George H. Kehm (Philadelphia: Fortress, 1970), p. 1.

10. Ibid., pp. 1–4.

11. Ibid., p. 13.

12. Ibid.

13. Ibid., p. 10.

14. Ibid., pp. 10–13. Pannenberg's use of apocalytic as a general phenomenon best understood not in terms of its details but as a view of his-

tory and a general horizon of expectation is supported by Koch's conclusion that apocalyptic is not only a literary genre but an *attitude of mind* that seeks to "interpret the course of history and to reveal the end of the world." Ringgren in Koch, *The Rediscovery of Apocalyptic*, p. 33. See also Wolfhart Pannenberg, "Redemptive Event and History," *Basic Questions in Theology*, vol. 1, p. 15.

15. Pannenberg, "Redemptive Event and History," pp. 18–35.

16. Wolfhart Pannenberg, *Jesus-God and Man*, trans. Lewis Wilkens and Duane A. Priebe (Philadelphia: Westminster, 1968), pp. 59–60.

17. Ibid., pp. 60–61, 65.

18. Ibid., pp. 67–69.

19. Wolfhart Pannenberg, "Theology and the Kingdom of God," *Theology and the Kingdom of God* (Philadelphia: Westminster, 1969), p. 53.

20. Pannenberg, *Jesus-God and Man*, p. 83.

21. Ibid., p. 85.

22. Ibid., pp. 86–88.

23. Ibid., pp. 106ff.

24. Jürgen Moltmann, *Theology of Hope*, trans. James W. Leitch (New York: Harper & Row, 1967), pp. 39–41.

25. Ibid., p. 103.

26. Ibid., pp. 103–4.

27. Ibid., pp. 133–34.

28. Ibid., p. 136.

29. Ibid., p. 137.

30. Jürgen Moltmann, "Religion, Revolution, and the Future," *Religion, Revolution, and the Future*, trans. Douglas Meeks (New York: Charles Scribner's Sons, 1969), pp. 21ff.

31. Moltmann, "What is 'New' in Christianity?" *Religion, Revolution, and the Future*, pp. 5–13.

32. Moltmann, *Theology of Hope*, pp. 192–93.

33. Ibid., p. 218.

34. Ibid., p. 142.

35. Moltmann, "The Future as New Paradigm of Transcendence," *Religion, Revolution, and the Future*, pp. 177–99.

36. Walter H. Capps, *Time Invades the Cathedral* (Philadelphia: Fortress, 1972), *passim*.

Chapter VI.
The Image of God and Eschatology

1. Walther Eichrodt, *Theology of the Old Testament*, vol. 2, trans. J. A. Baker (Philadelphia: Westminster, 1967), pp. 122–25; Friedrich-Wilhelm Eltester, *Eikon im Neuem Testament*, Beihefte zur Zeitschrift für die Neutestamentliche Wissenschaft, vol. 22 (Berlin: Töpelmann, 1958), pp. 13–16; Friedrich Horst, "Face to Face: The Biblical Doctrine of the Image of God," trans. John Bright, *Interpretation*, 4, 3 (1950), pp. 259–61; Edmond Jacob, *Theology of the Old Testament*, trans. Arthur J. Heathcote and Philip J. Allcock (New York: Harper & Row, 1958), pp. 167–68; Edvin Larsson, *Christus als Vorbild: Eine Untersuchung zu*

den paulinischen Tauf und Eikontexten, Acta Seminarii Neotestamentici Upsaliensis, vol. 23 (Uppsala: Almqvist & Wiksells, 1962), p. 116; N. W. Porteous, "Image of God," *Interpreter's Dictionary of the Bible,* vol. 2, pp. 682–85; Gerhard von Rad, *Genesis,* trans. John H. Marks (Philadelphia: Westminster, 1961), pp. 56–57. For a discussion of the relationship of the meaning of *tselem* as "shadow" (*Schattenbild*) in the Psalms to the concrete meaning indicated here see Karl Ludwig Schmidt, "Homo Imago Dei in Alten und Neuen Testament," *Eranos Jahrbuch,* 15 (1947-48), pp. 170–74. Schmidt's analysis concludes that the notion of image as "shadow" must ultimately be restricted to its occurrence in the two psalm passages.

2. Von Rad, *Genesis,* p. 587; Horst, "Face to Face," pp. 259–61.

3. Gerhard von Rad, *Old Testament Theology,* vol. 1, trans. D. M. G. Stalker (New York: Harper & Row, 1962), pp. 144–46; *Genesis,* pp. 56–57. "There are two passages in particular in P which prevent us from interpreting the theologoumenon of the divine likeness in a one-sidedly spiritual sense. In Gen. 5:1ff. reference is made to the physical progeny of the first man, and it is said of Seth, Adam's son, that he was begotten in the image and likeness of Adam. This statement is most important. It ensures the theological actuality for all generations of the witness to the divine likeness. For in itself the story of a being originally created in the divine likeness would be of no great significance for OT faith. In relation to the particular question, Gen. 5:3 tells us that the transmission of the divine likeness is thought of in terms of the physical sequence of generations and therefore obviously in a physical sense. The second passage is Gen. 9:6, where the prohibition of murder is grounded in the divine likeness. Here the thought is the same. Attack on man's body is violation of God's honor." Gerhard von Rad, *"eikon,"* trans. Geoffrey W. Bromiley, *Theological Dictionary of the New Testament,* vol. 2, ed. Gerhard Kittel, p. 391.

On the other side of the picture it is also not possible to restrict the image concept to a purely physical interpretation. Even Ludwig Köhler's attempt to explain the nature of the image purely on the basis of the concrete meaning of *tselem* points beyond a purely physical interpretation. The erect stature peculiar to man was stressed by the ancient writers as a key aspect of man's God-likeness. But it was also stressed that this stature indicates man's peculiar capacity to look upward to heaven, to God. Thus, even this purely physical approach to understanding *tselem* admits to the possibility of a deeper spiritual meaning. "Die Grundstelle der Imago-Dei-Lehre, Gen. 1:26," *Theologische Zeitschrift* 4 (1948), pp. 16–22.

Köhler, like most scholars, follows Paul Humbert's lead in the final analysis. Humbert, after careful and exhaustive word studies, concluded that the key term is *tselem* which indeed does refer to man's physical appearance. However, the Priestly writer introduced the more abstract notion of *demut* as its counterpart to avoid the conclusion that man was made as an exact copy of God's physical appearance. *Etudes sur le récit du paradis et de la chute dans la Genèse* (Neuchâtel, 1940), pp. 153–75.

4. Von Rad, *Old Testament Theology,* vol. 1, pp. 141–44; J. N. Thomas,

"What Is Man? The Biblical Doctrine of the Image of God," *Interpretation* 3 (April 1949), pp. 154–58; T. B. Maston, "Man: His Dignity and Worth," *Review and Expositor* 2 (July 1954), pp. 301–32.

5. Von Rad, *Old Testament Theology*, vol. 1, pp. 144–46. The difference between man and Yahweh is indicated in several ways. First of all, man is created, in von Rad's view, in the image of the *Elohim*, the heavenly beings. This understanding emerges in consideration of Ps. 8:5, which speaks of man as created "a little lower than the *Elohim*" taken together with the "let us" of 1:26 which von Rad believes refers to the council of heavenly beings and clearly reflects the P writer's attempt to refer the image to the *Elohim* rather than Yahweh directly. Secondly, there is an infinite difference in stature; Israel conceived of Yahweh as gigantic. Finally, man's sexual differentiation constitutes a considerable distinction from Yahweh for, despite the conception of the human form of Yahweh, sexuality is completely alien to Israel's understanding of him.

Von Rad places the Old Testament doctrine of the divine likeness in further perspective: "The distinctive meaning of the divine likeness in the OT can be understood only when we see in strict connection with a faith which is basically orientated by the sense of the greatest possible distance from God. The central point in OT anthropology is that man is dust and ashes before God and that he cannot stand before his holiness. Thus the witness to man's divine likeness plays no predominant role in the OT. It stands as it were on the margin of the whole complex." *"eikon," Theological Dictionary of the New Testament*, vol. 2, p. 390.

6. Horst, "Face to Face," pp. 259–64.

7. Von Rad, *Genesis*, pp. 57–58.

8. Eichrodt, *Theology of the Old Testament*, pp. 120–21; Thomas, "What Is Man?"; Maston, "Man"; Porteous, "Image of God."

9. Horst, "Face to Face," pp. 266–67.

10. The personal-relational character of the image of God as the unique feature of the human makeup is given further support by the larger context of Old Testament reflection on man. Man's creation for an I-Thou relationship with God and fellow human beings is documented in a sustained way by Walther Eichrodt in his discussion of the moral personalism of the law and the prophetic understanding of man's relationship to God. See *Man in the Old Testament*, trans. by R. Gregor Smith (Chicago: Allenson, 1951), *passim*.

11. Eichrodt, *Theology of the Old Testament*, vol. 2, pp. 126–27.

12. C. F. D. Moule, though differing from Eichrodt in that he practically equates the meaning of the image with the call to sovereignty, does offer a similar stress on the ethical responsibility that attends man's dominion over nature. In that Moule seeks a biblical theology for ecology, it is not surprising that he makes this his focal point. Accordingly, he proposes that the most satisfying interpretation of the image of God in man is one that sees its meaning as responsibility. If the authority of dominion is an ingredient of the image of God in man, then responsibility is its concomitant for "responsible authority is God-like." God is responsible to no one but he wields his absolute authority responsibly. Man is responsible to God to rule the rest of creation as responsibly as

God himself rules. That is, he is to rule nature according to the divine purpose. *Man and Nature in the New Testament*, Facet Books Biblical Series, 17, edited with Introduction by John Reumann (Philadelphia: Fortress, 1967), pp. 2–4.

13. Jacob, *Theology of the Old Testament*, p. 171.

14. Von Rad, *Genesis*, p. 94.

15. Jacob Jervell, *Imago Dei: Gen. 1, 26f. im Spätjudentum, in der Gnosis und in den paulinischen Briefen*, Forschungen zur Religion und Literatur des Alten und Neuen Testaments, Neue Folge, 58 (Göttingen: Vandenhoeck & Ruprecht, 1960), pp. 328ff., in discussing Rom. 1:23, is forced to the conclusion that the image of God is lost to sin because he equates the image with *doxa* and *doxa* with *dikaiosyne*. However, Larsson, *Christus als Vorbild*, p. 187 n., declines to identify *doxa* and *eikon* and also declines to equate *dikaiosyne* with *doxa*, pointing out that the concept of *dikaiosyne* is far too complicated in Paul to be so simply identified. The most that can be said is that *dikaiosyne* is a part of the *doxa* of man. So, also, Eltester, *Eikon*, pp. 153, 256, 263, points out that the loss of *doxa* in the Fall cannot be confirmed as equaling the loss of the image. Beyond this, two other considerations make it difficult to conclude that the New Testament speaks of a loss of the image: 1 Cor. 11:7 and Jas. 3:9 clearly speak of man in the image of God quite in accordance with the Old Testament; furthermore, nowhere in Colossians or in Paul do we find an explicit statement concerning the renewal of a lost image.

J. N. Thomas makes a similar analysis in his contention that the only passage that might be construed as indicating a restoration of something lost in the Fall is Col. 3:10 (Calvin, among others, understood it this way), which really only speaks of a change that will take place in Christ and not of a restoration. "What Is Man?"

For further refutation of the point that the loss of *doxa* in Rom. 1:23 is equal to the loss of the *eikon*, see M. D. Hooker, "Adam in Romans 1," New Testament Studies, 6 (1959–60), p. 305.

16. Larsson, *Christus als Vorbild*, pp. 123–24.

17. Schmidt, "Homo Imago Dei," pp. 182–87.

18. Helmut Thielicke, *Theological Ethics*, vol. 1, trans. and ed. William Lazareth (Philadelphia: Fortress, 1966), pp. 159, 167, 169.

19. Ibid.

20. Gustaf Wingren, *Man and the Incarnation*, trans. Ross Mackenzie (Philadelphia: Fortress, 1959), p. 32; see also pp. 23–33.

21. Eichrodt, *Theology of the Old Testament*, vol. 2, pp. 129–30.

22. Thomas, "What Is Man?" pp. 160–61.

23. Wingren, *Man and the Incarnation*.

24. Eichrodt, *Man in the Old Testament*, pp. 32ff.

25. Ibid., pp. 76–77.

26. Von Rad, *Old Testament Theology*, vol. 1, pp. 136–39.

27. Ibid., p. 137, emphasis mine.

28. Ibid., p. 139. See also Murray Campion, "The Origin of the World and Gen. 1–3," *Australian Biblical Review* 13 (1956), pp. 1–18. In this article designed to assess the influence of mythological thinking on the formation of the creation story in order to demonstrate how the OT

writers used myth as a means for expressing their historically oriented theology, Campion holds that the Jahwistic school extended the Exodus theology to a primeval origin of the world as a direct answer to the Canaanite myths concerning cosmos, creation, fertility, etc. "Thus the Jahwist sees a primal pattern of salvation history. Yahweh forms a garden from the chaotic desert; in this garden is placed man; the garden is the abode of God and hence sacred; man therefore must observe the sacred order established by God in the garden: covenant relationship man; man however disrupts this order by his independent action, which is sin, and so is reduced by God to a disturbed relationship with the universe." As with the later P document, which Campion believes is clearly under the influence of prophetic insights, the theme of Gen. 2–3 is that of Exodus, only with a universal dimension; hope in the future saving events of Yahweh in history.

29. Jervell, *Imago Dei*, pp. 173–97.

30. Ibid., pp. 214–18. See also Eltester, *Eikon*, p. 133. Eltester concurs in the judgment that it is only the resurrected and exalted Christ that is referred to as the *eikon tou Theou*. Concerning Christ as the image indicating Christ as the Revealer see also Gottfried Söhngen, "Die Biblishe Lehre von der Gottesbenbildichkeit des Menschen," *Münchner Theologische Zeitschrift* 2 (1951), pp. 59–61.

31. Jervell, *Imago Dei*, pp. 218–26; Schmidt, *Homo Imago Dei*, p. 190; Larsson, *Christus als Vorbild*, pp. 188–95; Söhngen, "Die Biblishe Lehre," pp. 48–49.

32. Larsson, *Christus als Vorbild*, pp. 293–323; Jervell, *Imago Dei*, pp. 256–92.

33. Robin Scroggs, *The Last Adam: A Study in Pauline Anthropology* (Philadelphia: Fortress, 1966), pp. 91ff.

34. Horst, "Face to Face," p. 270.

35. Jervell, *Imago Dei*, pp. 284–92.

36. Roy A. Harrisville, "The Concept of Newness in the New Testament" (Ph.D. dissertation, Princeton Theological Seminary, 1953), pp. 376–83.

37. Ibid., p. 383.

38. Ibid., p. 384. The *Urstand* idea of the old dogmaticians is a modification of the cyclic theory. However, ". . . any theory, however modified, which regards eschaton as equivalent of arche neglects the importance of the Incarnation as a totally new occurrence in history, its consequences for the historical process itself, and overlooks the Biblical utterances concerning the progression within eschatology itself." Consistent with this view, Harrisville points out, with impressive support from a number of commentators, that the new man in the Pauline epistles does not entail a return to the original.

39. Wolfhart Pannenberg, "Myth in Biblical and Christian Tradition," *The Idea of God and Human Freedom*, trans. R. A. Wilson (Philadelphia: Westminster, 1973), pp. 25–26.

40. Ibid., pp. 58ff.

41. Ibid., p. 60.

42. Ibid., pp. 60–66. The typological understanding of history, of course, provides Pannenberg with a biblical view of eschatology which is sup-

portive of his overall theology in its openness to the future and its orientation to the future. Though not stated specifically in this context, it would also seem that the dynamic of the typological view of history provides an underlying logic for the notion of the Christ event as a "proleptic" event. If, as Pannenberg states, projections of future hope can only be grounded in present experience or tradition—thus explaining the need for types from past events and traditions in Israel's expression of its eschatological hopes—then the logic for the Christ event as a prolepsis of the kingdom of God and, therefore, its nature as an eschatological event is assured. Although Christ cannot be considered as simply a type of something which is to come, his fulfillment of other eschatological types offers a proleptic eschatological revelation upon which to base Christian hope in the end. Proleptic event thus succeeds other significant events of Israel's past which were taken up in the typological view of history and eschatology before Christ. For the New Israel prolepsis functions in place of type.

Chapter VII.
Eschatological Man

1. Wolfhart Pannenberg, *Theology and the Kingdom of God* (Philadelphia: Westminster, 1969), pp. 55–60.
2. Ibid., p. 56.
3. Wolfhart Pannenberg, *The Idea of God and Human Freedom* (Philadelphia: Westminster, 1973), p. 109.
4. Ibid., pp. 99–115. See parallel thoughts in "The God of Hope," *Basic Questions in Theology*, vol. 2 (Philadelphia: Fortress), pp. 234ff.
5. Wolfhart Pannenberg, *What Is Man?*, trans. Duane A. Priebe (Philadelphia: Fortress, 1970), pp. 1–27; 41–53. See also *Jesus-God and Man* (Philadelphia: Westminster, 1968), pp. 191–95.
6. See Ernst Bloch, *Das Prinzip Hoffnung*, 2 vols. (Frankfurt: Suhrkamp Verlag, 1959); Bloch, *A Philosophy of the Future*, trans. John Cumming (New York: Herder and Herder, 1970); Bloch, *Man on His Own*, trans. E. B. Ashton (New York: Herder and Herder, 1970); Jürgen Moltmann, "Hope and Confidence: A Conversation with Ernst Bloch," *Religion, Revolution, and the Future* (New York: Charles Scribner's Sons, 1969), pp. 148–76; Carl Braaten, "Ernst Bloch's Philosophy of Hope," *The Futurist Option* (New York: Newman, 1970), pp. 59–78; Walter Capps, *Time Invades the Cathedral* (Philadelphia: Fortress, 1972), pp. 15–40; Pannenberg, "The God of Hope," *Basic Questions in Theology*, vol. 2, pp. 234–49.
7. Bloch, *A Philosophy of the Future*, p. 139.
8. Bloch, *Man on His Own*, p. 80, quoted in Capps, *Time Invades the Cathedral*, p. 29.
9. Capps, *Time Invades the Cathedral*, p. 28.
10. Other sources which might well be included in this discussion but which we shall have to pass by with a simple citation in this note would be Teilhard de Chardin, *The Phenomenon of Man* (New York: Harper & Row, 1965); Ray Hart, *Unfinished Man and the Imagination* (New York: Herder and Herder, 1968); Gordon D. Kaufman, *Systematic*

Theology: A Historicist Perspective (New York: Charles Scribner's Sons, 1968), especially the chapter "The *Imago Dei* as Man's Historicity" which was originally the title of an article published in *Journal of Religion* 36 (1956), pp. 157–68. Kaufman moves from an assertion of the historicality of all reality to the further asertion that man's being in the image of God is a reference to his historicity. There are two problems with Kaufman's position. He does succeed in construing reality in terms of the historical but only at the price of transcendence being eliminated altogether. There is no real hope here for there is no hope beyond the future horizon of death. Secondly, his historicist perspective is just that, a perspective. He lacks an ontology of history in which to ground his assertions, as he himself admits.

Of special note is the work of Daniel Day Williams who offers a sustained discussion of the image of God from the perspective of process thought. The whole question of the relationship of process thought and Pannenberg's theology is, of course, a matter of considerable interest to contemporary theology, though beyond the scope of this work. Daniel Day Williams, *The Spirit and Forms of Love* (New York: Harper & Row, 1968), pp. 131–43.

11. Pannenberg, *The Idea of God and Human Freedom,* p. 104.

12. Pannenberg, *Theology and the Kingdom of God,* p. 61.

13. Pannenberg, "The God of Hope," *Basic Questions in Theology,* vol. 2, p. 243.

14. Georges Florovsky attempts to demonstrate that the Greek Fathers placed more emphasis upon the idea of eschatology as "new creation" than upon a cyclical pattern of restoration. He cites Gregory Nazianzus particularly in this regard. His point is that the cyclical pattern of Aristotelian cosmology is destructive of eschatology as Christianity understands it. "Eschatology in the Patristic Age: An Introduction," *Studia Patristica,* vol. 2, ed. Kurt Aland and F. L. Cross, Texte und Untersuchen zur Geschichte der Altchristlichen Literatur (Berlin: Akademie Verlag), pp. 238–41.

15. Panagiotis Bratsiotis, "Genesis 1, 26 in der orthodoxen Theologie," *Evangelishe Theologie* 7–8 (1951–52), p. 293.

16. Pannenberg, "The God of Hope," *Basic Questions in Theology,* vol. 2, p. 240.

17. Pannenberg, *Theology and the Kingdom of God,* p. 69. Sin as resistance to the future has its counterpart in Heidegger's existential analytic of *Dasein. Dasein* chooses to live inauthentically when he refuses to project himself upon the ultimate horizon of his future and chooses instead the tranquilizing satisfaction of absorption in the impersonal world of things and in the depersonalizing world of the masses. This holding on to past satisfactions in a refusal of the future constitutes man's "fallenness." Martin Heidegger, *Being and Time,* trans. John Macquarrie and Edward Robinson (New York: Harper, 1962), pp. 219–24.

18. Pannenberg, *What Is Man?,* pp. 32ff.

19. Jacob Jervell, *Imago Dei: Gen. 1, 26f. im Spätjudentum, in der Gnosis und in den paulinischen Briefen* (Göttingen: Vandenhoeck & Ruprecht, 1960), pp. 233–36; Edvin Larsson, *Christus als Vorbild: Eine Untersuchung zu paulinischen Tauf und Eikontexten* (Uppsala: Almqvist

& Wiksells, 1962), pp. 197ff.; see also Gottfried Söhngen, "Die Biblishe Lehre von der Gottesbenbildlichkeit des Menschen" *Münchner Theologische Zeitschrift* 2 (1951), pp. 61ff. whose understanding of Col. 3:9ff. and Eph. 4:22–24 reflects the same general interpretation given here.

20. Jürgen Moltmann, *Theology of Hope* (New York: Harper & Row, 1967), p. 162. Notwithstanding his ahistorical theology, Rudolf Bultmann has understood the eschatological nature of the foundations of ethics in Pauline thought as well as anyone. Although the terms are ultimately loaded with different meaning his explanation of the freedom of the Christian in whom the Spirit dwells is much like the exposition we are working out here. The Spirit is mediated in baptism together with the new creation in the image, as we have pointed out. For Bultmann this life in the Spirit is demonstrated in the fact that it gives the believer freedom and opens up the future, the eternal life. "For freedom is nothing else than being open for the genuine future, letting one's self be determined by the future. So Spirit may be called the power of futurity." *Theology of the New Testament*, vol. 1 (New York: Charles Scribner's Sons, 1951), pp. 334–35.

21. Karl Barth, *Church Dogmatics*, vol. 3, 1, authorized trans. by G. T. Thompson (New York: Charles Scribner's Sons, 1936), pp. 183ff, 195ff.

22. In an article which reflects the sort of perspective on the image of God that I have been developing here, Pannenberg makes the connection between the proleptic revelation of our true humanity in Christ and the requirement to love our fellowman. See, "Der Mensch—Ein Ebenbild Gottes?" pp. 36–37.

23. Pannenberg, *Theology and the Kingdom of God,* p. 126.

Chapter VIII.
Grounding the Good

1. Richard H. Hiers, *Jesus and Ethics* (Philadelphia: Westminster, 1968); *The Kingdom of God in the Synoptic Tradition* (Gainesville, Fla.: University of Florida Press, 1970); *The Historical Jesus and the Kingdom of God,* University of Florida Humanities Monograph Number 38 (Gainesville, Fla.: University of Florida Press, 1973).

2. Hiers, *The Historical Jesus and the Kingdom of God,* pp. 16–24.

3. This stance comes through in all the three works by Hiers cited above in note 1. In *Jesus and Ethics* he especially takes to task Harnack and Schweitzer for their attempts to detach Jesus' ethics from his eschatology, and he is critical of Bultmann and Dodd for translating Jesus' eschatological world view into more congenial categories of existentialism and Platonism respectively; see chaps. 1–4.

4. "At all events, if we wish to know anything about the historical Jesus, we shall have to turn to the historical, eschatological Jesus." Hiers, *The Historical Jesus and the Kingdom of God,* p. 117.

5. Hiers, *Jesus and Ethics,* pp. 165–68.

6. Hiers, *The Historical Jesus and the Kingdom of God,* p. 115.

7. Norman Metzler, "The Ethics of the Kingdom" (Ph.D. dissertation, University of Munich, 1971), p. 202.

8. Ibid.

9. Ibid., pp. 221ff.

10. Ibid., pp. 414–15.

11. Ibid., p. 416.

12. Wolfhart Pannenberg, *Theology and the Kingdom of God* (Philadelphia: Westminster, 1969), p. 106.

13. Joseph Fletcher, *Moral Responsibility: Situation Ethics at Work* (Philadelphia: Westminster, 1967), p. 14.

14. Brand Blanshard, "The Impasse in Ethics—and a Way Out," *Readings in Ethical Theory,* ed. Wilfred Sellers and John Hospers, 2d ed. (New York: Appleton-Century-Crofts, 1970), p. 301.

15. Pannenberg, *Theology and the Kingdom of God,* pp. 109–10.

16. See Paul Tillich, "The Protestant Principle and the Proletarian Situation," *The Protestant Era* (Chicago: The University of Chicago Press, 1957), pp. 165–70.

17. Tillich, *Systematic Theology,* vol. 3 (Chicago: The University of Chicago Press, 1951), pp. 355–56.

18. Pannenberg, *Theology and the Kingdom of God,* p. 111.

19. Ibid.

20. Wolfhart Pannenberg, "Facts of History and Christian Ethics," *Dialog* 8 (Autumn 1969), p. 290.

21. Ibid., p. 293. See also Jürgen Moltmann's chapter "The Understanding of History in Christian Social Ethics," *Hope and Planning,* trans. Margaret Clarkson (New York & London: Harper & Row, 1971), pp. 101–29 for his critique and alternative to an ethics of orders.

22. In his critique of transcendental two kingdoms thought, Paul Tillich finds fault with its restriction of the scope of grace to the exclusion of the sociopolitical and other historical structures. In contrast he points out that the symbol of the kingdom of God includes four characteristics: political, social, personalistic, and universal. As such it includes the arrival of the peace and justice of God as well as the fulfillment of the humanity of every individual. It is a promise for the future as well as a judgment upon the ambiguities of the present. In its universality none of the dimensions of life is eliminated from salvation. *Systematic Theology,* vol. 3, pp. 355–59.

Chapter IX.
Deciding the Right

1. Paul Ramsey, *Deeds and Rules in Christian Ethics* (New York: Charles Scribner's Sons, 1967), particularly pp. 104–22.

2. James M. Gustafson, "Context Versus Principles: A Misplaced Debate in Christian Ethics," *Christian Ethics and the Community* (Philadelphia: United Church Press, 1971), chap. 3.

3. See E. L. Long's important article, "Soteriological Implications of Norm and Context," *Norm and Context in Christian Ethics,* ed. Gene H. Outka and Paul Ramsey (New York: Charles Scribner's Sons, 1968), pp. 265–95, especially his criticism of legalism.

4. In an earlier article, "The Third Use of the Law and Constructive Ethics," *Currents in Theology and Mission,* 2, 1 (February 1975), pp.

35–40, I offered in brief form and from a somewhat different perspective the same moral theory under discussion here. However, in that context I appropriated the term "summary rule" as a good description of my own theory of rules. In doing so, I transformed the concept summary rule into something considerably different from the way in which it is customarily used. Since that time, I have decided not to use that term. The criticism of summary rule theory that I offer here is, thus, made in terms of its normal usage in some forms of situationism, not in terms of the way I used it in the article cited above. For my own suggestion on the use of rules in Christian ethics I offer here the term "general rule," a term used by Paul Ramsey, *Deeds and Rules,* pp. 13ff., which appears to correspond more closely to what I have in mind.

5. See again Long, "Soteriological Implications."

6. See Helmut Thielicke's criticism of legalistic interpretations of the commands in the Sermon on the Mount and his discussion of the role of commandment in conflict situations. *Theological Ethics,* vol. 1 (Philadelphia: Fortress, 1966), pp. 384ff. and 609ff.

7. See W. D. Ross's discussion of *prima facie* duties and actual duties in *The Right and the Good* (Oxford: The Clarendon Press, 1930).

8. John C. Bennett, *Christian Ethics and Social Policy* (New York: Charles Scribner's Sons, 1946), p. 77.

9. Ibid.

10. Ibid., p. 78.

11. Ibid., p. 88.

12. Harmon Smith, *Ethics and the New Medicine* (Nashville: Abingdon, 1970), p. 121, lists as examples of middle axioms in the field of medical ethics the following moral guidelines suggested by Drs. J. R. Elkington and Eugene D. Robin to give direction in organ transplantation: "1. Compassionate concern for the patient as a total person is the primary goal of the physician and investigator. 2. Organ transplantation should have some reasonable possibility of clinical success. 3. The transplant must be undertaken only with an acceptable therapeutic goal as its purpose. 4. Risk to the healthy donor of an organ must be kept low, but such risk should not be a contraindication to the voluntary offer of an organ by an informed donor. 5. There must be complete honesty with the patient and his family, including every benefit of available general medical knowledge and of specific information concerning transplantation. 6. Each transplantation should be conducted under a protocol which ensures the maximum possible addition to scientific knowledge. 7. Careful, intensive, and objective evaluation of results of independent observers is mandatory. 8. A careful, accurate conservative approach to the dissemination of information to the news media is desirable."

13. George F. Thomas, *Christian Ethics and Moral Philosophy* (New York: Charles Scribner's Sons, 1955), pp. 440–44.

14. Ernst Käsemann, " 'The Righteousness of God' in Paul," *New Testament Questions of Today* (Philadelphia: Fortress, 1969), pp. 180–81.

Index

179